Soc Sec p 96

THE WEALTH MAZE

JOE CHORNYAK

THE
WEALTH
MAZE

SECRETS FOR NAVIGATING
THE LABYRINTH OF LIFE

ForbesBooks

Published by ForbesBooks, Charleston, South Carolina.
Member of Advantage Media Group.

ForbesBooks is a registered trademark, and the ForbesBooks colophon is a trademark of Forbes Media, LLC.

Printed in the United States of America.

10 9 8 7 6 5 4 3 2 1

ISBN: 978-1-946633-62-0
LCCN: 2020922362

Book design by Megan Elger.

This custom publication is intended to provide accurate information and the opinions of the author in regard to the subject matter covered. It is sold with the understanding that the publisher, Advantage|ForbesBooks, is not engaged in rendering legal, financial, or professional services of any kind. If legal advice or other expert assistance is required, the reader is advised to seek the services of a competent professional.

Advantage Media Group is proud to be a part of the Tree Neutral® program. Tree Neutral offsets the number of trees consumed in the production and printing of this book by taking proactive steps such as planting trees in direct proportion to the number of trees used to print books. To learn more about Tree Neutral, please visit **www.treeneutral.com**.

Since 1917, Forbes has remained steadfast in its mission to serve as the defining voice of entrepreneurial capitalism. ForbesBooks, launched in 2016 through a partnership with Advantage Media Group, furthers that aim by helping business and thought leaders bring their stories, passion, and knowledge to the forefront in custom books. Opinions expressed by ForbesBooks authors are their own. To be considered for publication, please visit **www.forbesbooks.com**.

To my Mom, Cecilia Chornyak, and my Dad, Mike Chornyak, who shared with me their strong faith in God and who taught me so much about working hard, trying to always do it right the first time, and living life as a true giver to others.

CONTENTS

CHAPTER 1

Introduction: Why I Wrote This Book and What It Can Do for You

nsurance planning. Risk management. Wills, trusts, estate planning. College education planning. Retirement planning. Succession planning. In today's complex financial landscape, planning is the vehicle that will deliver you to your ultimate destination—if you've done it properly. That's why I wrote this book. I wanted to simplify, explore, and explain the financial industry as honestly as I would if you were sitting across the desk from me.

Maybe you have questions about your own finances and how they're being handled. Perhaps you're just starting out and aren't sure how to begin. I wrote this book so that you'd have a guide. I wrote it to provide that second opinion you may have been seeking. The more you understand about the many moving parts of the financial industry, the better equipped you'll be to make sound decisions. People make poor choices about their finances every day, not because they lack intelligence but because they lack the behind-the-scenes information I'm going to share with you here.

ARE YOU WORKING WITH A FINANCIAL PLANNER OR A SALESPERSON?

Recently, I sat down with two new clients and had a conversation that was similar to many I've had in my forty-plus-year career. Because I have to be an educator in meetings like these, I had the unpleasant task of showing this married couple why their financial plan wasn't what they thought it was. The husband felt terrible and blamed himself. It wasn't his fault, and I told him that. The salesperson, someone he trusted, had just told him pieces and parts of what he wanted him to hear so that the salesperson could make a bigger commission.

I told this couple what I've told many people over the years when I see some of the products they've been sold. "Look," I said, "the person you're working with is looking out for number one. The problem is you're not number one. The salesperson is."

Unfortunately, that happens in the financial industry and other industries when greed takes over. I told that husband not to beat himself up because somebody wasn't straightforward—and in my opinion, wasn't fulfilling their fiduciary duty and responsibility to do what was right. Then, once we got that out of the way, the couple and I created a plan that put them first.

I wrote this book because I can't sit down with you in my office the way I did with them. I wrote it so that the next time someone tries to sell you a financial product, you'll know the right questions to ask. I wrote it so that you can feel secure that you have a plan and not a promise. And just as important, I wrote this book because after all these years, I am still passionate about this industry and the role I play in it.

HELPING PEOPLE

Later, I'll share more about my values and where they originated. For now, I'll just say that I believe there are givers and takers in this world, and I'm a giver. Perhaps because of my early life when I had very little, I wanted to help people. But I also wanted to eat. I needed a job. Then I saw one of those ads that were so prevalent in the mid-1970s.

How would you like to be your own boss? You name your own hours. You come and go as you please. You don't have to answer to anybody, and you can make a lot of money.

I didn't know that dream job being described was insurance sales, but I went on an interview. I knew little about life insurance or cash value life insurance, but the part of the interview that intrigued me was this: "The harder you work, the more you can make," the company reps said. My parents taught me a very strong work ethic, and I thought if working hard was what it took, I'd be just fine.

However, the more I came to learn about the business and how it worked, and being mathematically inclined, I crunched some numbers and said to myself, "Some of these pieces and parts just don't make a lot of sense." It all boiled down to what my mom taught me as a kid: "Always treat people the way you want to be treated, and you'll never have to say you're sorry."

So I had to be honest about what I was selling, and I tried to figure out whether this product was what I would want someone to sell to me. More often than not, it wasn't. I wouldn't have bought that cash value life insurance policy because it was too expensive. Furthermore, if you did the math, it really wasn't a great investment. In those early days, whether I was working in insurance or investments, I always tried to do what was right for the client, not what made me the most money. That's one reason I didn't stay a salesperson for long, and it's an important reason I have had such a successful business all these years.

The insurance company I worked for had us ask questions, but the approach was built around the idea of trying to get the customer to buy cash value building whole life insurance. "If you were to pass away today, how would your spouse be left?" "How much do you want to leave your spouse and your children?" And "How much life insurance do you have?" Back in the 1970s, the norm wasn't about saving for retirement; it was about trying to peddle life insurance. The idea was to sell the individuals as much as possible.

All the insurance companies had any number of products, and they insisted that the average person on the street needed to have millions and millions of dollars of life insurance. Our job was to figure out how much they could afford and then sell them a life insurance policy within their budget that paid us the biggest commission. That's how we made a living, and I never felt comfortable with it.

I started out in the insurance industry in 1976, and in 1978, I obtained my securities license to market mutual funds and variable annuity products through that same insurance company. At that time, it was trying to expand, so we could start asking people more questions about investments. Then my life took a turn in the right direction. In 1979, I started reading about something called financial planning and becoming a Certified Financial Planner (CFP®).

After reading what articles I could find and doing research, I knew that was a career path I wanted to take because it was truly helping people. Instead of trying to peddle low-yielding, high-cash value, high-commission, whole life insurance, financial planning was looking at the world in a different way. In simple terms, it was trying to figure out the best way of looking at not only what would happen if a client got hit by a bus but also what would happen if they lived to retirement. I was fascinated by the idea of looking at someone's life from a multilevel standpoint over different time periods and timelines. I had found my calling.

In 1980, while working on my certification, I left the insurance organization I was with, went to work for a stockbrokerage firm, and got my full securities license with that firm. Soon it became apparent to me that stockbrokers were often no different than insurance agents or car salespeople; they were churn and burn—that is, the practice of making excessive brokerage trades to rack up commissions.

This was a prominent firm, yet I remember being in the office three nights a week when the branch manager would hand out a script. We were supposed to make sixty to seventy phone calls, read off this script, and try to get somebody to buy this stock or that bond because it was the latest and the greatest.

Interestingly enough, three months later—whether that investment went up, went down, or laid flat—it was time to sell. Why? Because every time the customer bought, the salesperson made a commission. And every time the customer sold, the salesperson made a commission. Oh, and there was something else. When the customer sold, they had cash, so there was another script to get them to buy something else. Again, to make yet another commission!

As a planner type, I didn't fit that mold because I believed that you make your serious money by investing for the long haul, not the short haul. So I left, finished my coursework, and obtained my certification in 1982. At the time, once you met all the accreditation requirements and passed all the exams, you received your CFP® license number in chronological order. My license number is 5,311. There weren't many of us around back in those days.

THE BOTTOM LINE

To this day, I believe—and I believe our firm's success proves—that if you do what's best for the client, if you do what's right, in the end, it will come back tenfold. Today we have a staff of eleven. Bob Mauk, a CFP®, has been with me since the mid-1980s. My son, Joe Jr., also a CFP®, likes to tell people he's been in the business fifty years, but that's actually how long he's been around. (He's actually been in the business twenty-seven years.) We have a CPA, an enrolled agent, a tax department, and administrative staff members with a variety of skills and experience. We're a comprehensive planning firm, and we truly do A-to-Z planning, from start to finish.

> To this day, I believe— and I believe our firm's success proves—that if you do what's best for the client, if you do what's right, in the end, it will come back tenfold.

A lot of folks say they do that, but the reality is that many know how to do only one thing. It may be investments, it may be insurance, or it may be taxes. We can drill down deep in any one of these areas because we're knowledgeable in all of these areas. We do investment planning and investment implementation. We do income tax planning and, in many cases, coordinate the preparation of those returns with several outside CPA firms we work with. We do insurance planning and risk management. We do wills and trusts and estate planning with a law firm we've used for more than thirty years. We do retirement planning, we do college education planning, and we do succession planning. We also partner with an outside CPA firm and an outside law firm in order to provide the depth and breadth of expertise our clients need.

When we take on a new client, we leave no stone unturned

because all these pieces are integrated, and I don't think you can deal with just one of them in a vacuum. You have to deal with all the pieces of the financial puzzle in order to see what the whole picture will—or better yet, should—look like.

The help and guidance we provide are based on lessons learned over decades in terms of trying to help people get a sense for what questions they should be asking and what kind of red flags they should be looking for. That's what I want to offer you in this book.

I also want to offer you hope. As I finish this book, our country and the world are dealing with a pandemic and the related financial ramifications. It's happened before, and, in my opinion, was worse in 2008—because we didn't know when it would end. With this one, we know there's a light at the end of the tunnel. And that light is when the virus ends. I recently spoke about our economic situation with Bill Heffner, a friend and client. He shared with me a quote— one of many—from his late father, Ralph Heffner, and I want to share it with you: *"Everybody has a little gold dust in their eyes. Just don't let it turn into nuggets—don't get nuggets in your eyes. Be careful because greed sets in."*

That quote gave me chills because of its wisdom, immediacy, and timeliness. *Don't get nuggets in your eyes.* So true. It is important to invest for the long term and to be patient during periods of market volatility. When the stock market goes up and up, people tend to want to get in. They get "nuggets" in their eyes, and they operate based on fear and greed, not sound financial wisdom.

We'll talk more about that in this book, and I'm also going to share information on stock picking, mutual funds, and index

> It is important to invest for the long term and to be patient during periods of market volatility.

funds. I'll point out common investor mistakes—from thinking the wrong way about investing, to lack of diversification, to emotional investing decisions—you may be making. Just as important, we're going to talk about quality of life because, when all is said and done, that really is the bottom line. So, let's get started by looking at some of today's challenges.

CHAPTER 2

Your Investment Challenges

Maybe you've just inherited a large sum of money and aren't sure how or where to invest it. Perhaps you're looking at retirement and wondering if you'll ever have enough to retire. Maybe you just have that feeling in the pit of your stomach that you want someone you trust to tell you you're doing the right thing. In the previous chapter, I told you about a married couple who came to me with a portfolio that was designed to enhance not their future but the financial gain of their advisor. This couple found out that they weren't doing the right thing, which is never a pleasant discovery. But once they got over the initial realization, they also found out how to overcome the challenges they faced. You can do the same.

Most of the new clients who consult with our firm face investment challenges. Perhaps you can relate to that. In today's complex market, how are you supposed to manage your own financial planning when you are not a financial planner? How are you supposed to trust so-called experts when you don't have an inside understanding of the industry? First, it's important to give yourself permission to go into learning mode. For now, let's just start with the basics, and the first one is figuring out what type of investor you are. In my decades of working with a wide range of customers, I've identified three main types along with the mistakes each type makes.

Different clients have different needs, but regardless of circumstance, most people ask similar questions and have similar goals. We will look at each of these issues in turn in this chapter.

WHAT'S YOUR TYPE?

Risk Averse

If you're this type, you've been managing your money by yourself and reached the point where your assets have grown enough that you no longer feel comfortable making your own decisions and need professional help. Growth means higher stakes. Volatility, even though it is a necessity to any serious investor, can create self-doubt.

Disappointed with Rate of Return

Maybe you've been working with a financial advisor, insurance agent, or stockbroker, and yet you feel that your rate of return is below average, and you don't know why. The answer might be that you're paying way too much in fees and expenses (often buried inside the particular investment vehicles being used).

Involved in Job Transition

Perhaps you worked for many years, and your employer has now either merged with another company or downsized. If you follow the trend of most individual investors in this scenario, you probably have tied up the bulk of your money in a 401(k) invested in mutual funds your employer picked or in company stock, have a pension plan with a lump sum payout, and/or have stock options or restricted stock in that company. Once your employment with the company ends, the challenge of managing these assets falls to you.

Each of these types is questioning if they could be doing better, and they are worried about what will happen to them if they don't.

When we do an initial assessment with a new client, we see the same common mistakes pop up. Here are a few:

- Highly concentrated, risky investment portfolios (oftentimes in passively managed index funds and company stock)

- Life insurance and annuities with high surrender charges used as investment vehicles

- High annual advisory fees, which may please the advisor but reduce the client's rate of return

Those examples demonstrate how people can have good intentions but make poor choices. Doing nothing can be as dangerous as doing the wrong thing. Some people fall into the following two categories:

- Those who don't want to pay any fees. They try to manage their own investments without realizing they don't have the expertise or the time needed to monitor those investments on a regular basis. Furthermore, they don't realize how their emotions get in the way of making sound objective investment decisions.

- Those who have an emotional connection to their investments. Some people don't want to let go of their company stock, even if it is not furthering their financial goals. Others inherited a portfolio of stocks and bonds or mutual funds when a family member passed away and are so emotionally tied to the portfolio that they do nothing with it.

Most of these people do want a better quality of life and enough money to retire. Unfortunately, figuring out how to achieve their goals is a challenge because they don't know how to think about money. And hard decisions often need to be made. That is something I'm going to teach you in this book. Before we do that, let's look at current trends and how you might fit into them.

INDIVIDUAL INVESTOR TRENDS TODAY

Mutual Funds and Index Funds

Today many people put their money into actively managed mutual funds or passively managed index funds. In the early days of individual investor trading, mutual funds were created as a professionally managed investment fund to pool money from many investors in order to purchase a diversified collection of securities.

Here's what they can invest in:

- Stocks

- Bonds

- Cash

- Other assets

These underlying security types—holdings—form one mutual fund, also called a portfolio.

Indices have been used since at least the late nineteenth century to measure either broad markets or different segments of the broader markets. For example, the S&P 500 index is intended to provide a broad measure of the market as a whole based on the market capitalizations of five hundred large companies having common stock listed on the NYSE or NASDAQ. A market sector index is the weighted average of the price of several stocks in a particular section of the stock market. Index values help investors track changes in market value over long periods of time and are often used as a benchmark for their own portfolio returns.

Over time, a mutual fund that aimed to mirror an index emerged. This became known as an index fund, which at face value can sound attractive to the inexperienced investor. Costs are low, but this is because, unlike mutual funds that are actively managed, index funds are not managed. They work on autopilot to mirror the market. An index fund is the ultimate passive investment, a formula-driven type of system. Since success is measured against the index that is mirrored and the cost structure is lower, it should be no surprise that many studies indicate that index funds outperform most managed funds.

Fortunately, you do not need to choose to either invest in an index fund or invest in all the managed funds out there. You can be selective.

Good mutual fund management companies have analysts and researchers who visit companies and talk to CEOs and the senior management of those companies. They have teams of forensic accountants who scour financial statements looking for irregularities. They have teams of retired CIA and FBI interrogators who teach their managers, analysts, and researchers how to read body language, voice inflection, and eye movement in an effort to gain insight into whether the answers CEOs are providing to questions are telling the whole story. Reducing risk through active management, therefore, comes at a cost.

In my opinion, this cost is worth it. It may add a bit of subjectivity, but it is an informed subjectivity. It may be hard to match an index fund during a broad upswing, just based on full investment, lower costs, and the mathematical result of the index fund owning all of the winners, but when market rises are more selective or markets fall or are disrupted, it would seem to make more sense to know that someone has given some intelligent thought to what you actually own. Because we know for sure that on the way down, the index also owns all the losers. An index fund is designed to avoid under-performing the index. It is not designed to manage risk. I think the question becomes, Would you rather have your investments selected and monitored by well-trained and well-informed professionals or based on a list created by a financial publisher? The list may show good results compared to most funds, but I would still rather know my investments have been chosen with some scrutiny and continue to be monitored by professionals—professionals who often do, in fact, have long-term track records of outperforming the indices.

Stock Picking

As I mentioned before, many individual investors try to pick stocks on their own, which is challenging. They have to do their own research, while professional money managers have access to research and analysis. You'd be unrealistic to think you could do as well without that level of research and analysis, not to mention experience.

Over the years, we have come across individual investors who have been picking individual stocks and bonds. When they come to us initially, part of our comprehensive planning includes looking at tax returns and investment statements in prior years. We analyze their performance and their choices over time, looking at the stocks that were winners and those that were losers. We've discovered that clients who are picking stocks often remember the winners that they held onto, and they forget the losers that they sold. They have short memories when it comes to what did not work out and long memories when it comes to what did. This selective recall is human nature, but it prevents you from honestly reviewing your overall success—or lack of it.

This approach to portfolio management on a day-to-day basis is problematic because the investor is not looking at each stock and analyzing the company the way active managers do before making subjective decisions to buy or sell. The typical investor lacks the time, the research tools, and/or the expertise to do so.

> We've discovered that clients who are picking stocks often remember the winners that they held onto, and they forget the losers that they sold.

If you would like to dabble in the market yourself, then take a slice of your investment pot and consider it gambling money. If an investment does well, that's great, but if it does not, you've gambled (and lost) only one slice of the investment pie. The rest has been invested with professionals who are taking different approaches to actively managing money in broadly diversified stocks. Not only does this approach minimize risk, but it also highlights how a slice of the pie compares to slices that are being actively managed by professionals.

COMMON INDIVIDUAL INVESTOR MISTAKES TODAY

Earlier I listed the three categories in which many individual investors fall. These three types are the Risk Averse, the Disappointed, and the In Transition. Many of them face common challenges in the marketplace today. These mistakes generally involve thinking the wrong way about money, failing to diversify, failing to set goals and objectives or prioritize, failing to ensure the goals of their investment vehicle align with their own goals, investing emotionally, or procrastinating. Let's take a look at these mistakes.

Thinking the Wrong Way about Money

Focusing on rate of return alone is dangerous. In fact, it's the biggest mistake people make when thinking about money because it overlooks how much risk one takes in an effort to get that rate of return.

Studies have shown that when certain assets are doing well, investors move all their money into those assets. However, when these stocks pull back, which is inevitable in the business cycle, those investors go into panic mode. They get out of the market and wait for an upswing before they are comfortable enough to reinvest their money.

Many people were so badly burned in the financial meltdown from October 2007 to March 2009 that they kept their money liquid because they lost trust or confidence in themselves and/or the market. They no longer felt they knew what to do with their money, and fearing another pullback, they stayed out and lost out when the market rebounded.

As I'm sure you've heard before, markets are driven by greed and fear. People tend to put all their money into the markets when it's high because they don't want to miss out on the market run-up. Then, when markets drop, they become afraid of losing their money and take it out of the markets. We will discuss this more in chapter 11.

Failing to Diversify

Related to mistakes in thinking about money is the mistake of nondiversification.

People often end up with a highly concentrated portfolio because they invest in the company for which they work. If they work in a company, believe in a company, get a paycheck from a company, and live and breathe that company, they often lose objectivity and forget that every company, sooner or later, makes a mistake. Numerous

Fortune 500 companies have. At one time, people believed General Electric was the greatest company on the planet, but they lost a lot of money when GE's stock price was cut in half. McClatchy, once the second-largest newspaper chain in the country, founded in 1857 in Sacramento, California, declared bankruptcy in 2020. Publisher of the *Miami Herald, Kansas City Star,* and other regional dailies, McClatchy took on large debt with its $4.5 billion takeover of Knight Ridder in 2006, but the digital boom won. Times change, and the way we invest must change as well.

Another failure-to-diversify scenario emerges from within the market itself. In 1998 and 1999, at the height of the technology boom, many investors focused on internet stocks, technology, and telecommunications. At the time, well-diversified, actively managed portfolios did not do as well as those invested in a basket of high-tech companies. A client came to us in late 1999 and said, "I understand diversification, but an acquaintance of mine is a professor at Duke University, in the finance area in the business school, where he's been modeling these technology stocks. And he's been doing significantly better than my portfolio."

The client had been doing well by following our advice and had been earning returns of 10 percent on average over many years, but enticed by tech-stock returns, he decided to move his account. Then the tech bubble burst. Two years later, he was left with only 20 percent of his original investment. He let greed get in the way of common sense. He was so focused on rate of return that he ended up with a portfolio highly concentrated in one industry, which cost him dearly. Holding 20 percent, 30 percent, 40 percent, or 50 percent of your money in a single stock or a single index or industry sets you up for a fall. The key here is to remember that broad diversification is your friend.

Failing to Set Goals

Let's make that not setting *realistic* goals. That's one of the most common mistakes individual investors make. The financial world is complex. People aren't taught in school how to manage their financial affairs. Because of technology today, paychecks are automatically deposited in the bank, and bills are automatically paid. This allows people to ignore their finances, which means they put off planning for their future, for retirement, or for a major expense.

Failure to prioritize, or failure to know what to prioritize, is another common investment mistake. Many individual investors focus on the rate of return before looking at their investment goals and objectives. The first questions you ask should not be, "What is my rate of return, and how much money can I make?" but "What am I trying to accomplish, and why am I trying to accomplish that?"

Is your goal building a nest egg for educating children or donating to a philanthropic organization, or is it accumulating enough so that you can retire, live comfortably, and pass something on to your children?

Once you know what you want and why, you can decide how to go about achieving those goals. We will discuss this in more detail in future chapters.

Once you establish goals, you can buy individual stocks and bonds or invest in a portfolio of diversified mutual funds. The issue then becomes deciding on which mutual funds in which to invest. Again, a mistake many people make is going with the ones that are showing the highest rate of return.

Failure to Align Personal and Investment Vehicle Goals

When deciding to invest in a mutual fund, the first questions you need to ask yourself are: What are the goals and objectives of the particular mutual fund? Are they buying stocks or bonds or both? If they are buying stocks, are they buying large blue-chip companies, medium-size companies, or small companies? Are they buying companies that take all their profits and plow them back to grow the company, or are they taking some of their profits and paying the shareholders in the form of dividends? Are they investing in companies that are head-quartered in the United States or in other parts of the world? How a mutual fund is investing money has a direct effect on the ultimate rate of return an investor will see. If how the money is invested isn't a factor, then the investor ends up taking far more risk than is needed to reach their goals.

A second factor to assess when investing in a mutual fund is who is managing the money. As I mentioned previously, index funds are passively managed based on the particular index that they are mirroring. The portfolio manager does not have the ability to make subjective decisions on what to buy and sell. For an actively managed fund, rate of return is related to how a fund is being managed and who is managing it. For example, if the manager has been managing a fund for two years and the investment decision is based on the ten-year rate of return, then it is being based on the performance of the person who preceded the current manager. It's also important for you to check whether the managers have significant amounts of their own money invested in the mutual fund they manage. Do they have skin in the game?

Another factor to assess when deciding to invest in a mutual fund is whether it is highly concentrated or well diversified across different industries for the reasons we discussed earlier in this chapter.

The answers to these questions—how it's being managed, who is managing it, and how diversified it is—can steer the investor clear of common mistakes. At this point, they can look at rate of return, which we'll discuss in more detail later in this book.

Emotional Investing

No one likes to lose money, but this fear leads to investment mistakes. It is important to remember that no industry goes up forever. Every industry has a cycle. We do not know when that cycle is going to turn. When oil was one hundred dollars a barrel, everyone loved energy; then it dropped to under thirty dollars a barrel, and everyone hated energy. The truth is that there is value in thirty dollars a barrel, but individual investors tend to buy high, and then when they get burned, they don't want to go back. That's where emotions get in the way of making rational decisions. When it comes to investing, emotions have an adverse effect on investor outcomes.

Procrastination

Another common mistake the individual investor makes is procrastinating. In fact, procrastination is probably one of the biggest reasons why investors do not do well. They do not take action. They may not be comfortable where they are, but still, they bury their heads in the sand. They put it off until tomorrow, and tomorrow turns into ten or fifteen years. It's not unusual for someone to say to us after our first meeting when we've done an assessment, "Gosh, I wish I'd come to see you ten years ago." (So do we.)

> Procrastination is probably one of the biggest reasons why investors do not do well. They do not take action.

Because we understand the challenges that exist in the marketplace and in the individual lives of investors, we focus on what is inherently one simple goal: helping clients accumulate and grow their assets so that at some point in time they can draw a line in the sand and say, "From this day forward, I'm working because I want to, not because I need to." Putting this financial plan in place changes the whole complexion of an investor's outlook on their career and on their life because the financial burden is lifted. In the process of lifting it, they learn to think the right way about their money and the goals they have around spending it and investing it.

TAKEAWAY

→ Many challenges face the individual investor in today's marketplace. Some of these relate to the investment vehicles available or recent trends, and some relate to mistakes the individual investors tend to make for the various reasons discussed in this chapter.

→ Understanding your goals allows you to assess whether you are diversified or too concentrated. You can see how much of your net worth is tied up in the company you work for or in indices or funds that may or may not be in your best financial interest.

→ The first question every investor should ask is where they want to be in three or five years or even how long they want to work. If you have not asked this question, it may be time to sit with a spouse or partner, talk this through, and devise a plan. We will talk about the ways to do that in later chapters. First, I want to share with you how the values of our company were derived from my early life experiences.

CHAPTER 3

Lessons—and Values—Learned

n the introduction of this book, I mentioned that childhood taught me values that have stayed with me throughout my life and career, and that I'm proud to say I've passed along to those, including my son, who work with me. I believe those values have helped me avoid some of the common mistakes others make.

LESSONS FROM CHILDHOOD

I was born and raised in humble beginnings in a small town about twenty miles outside of Pittsburgh, Pennsylvania. My father's education ended at the tenth grade and my mother's at the eleventh. My father worked hard at two jobs to support the family. Unfortunately, he was addicted to gambling, which created financial troubles in our household. These early experiences, good and bad, were formative, and I was fortunate enough to develop some values that have become an integral part of my life and business today.

The Value of Proper Planning

As a child, I couldn't do the things other kids in the neighborhood did. Other families had two cars. They could go on nice vacations. If we wanted anything, we could not expect it just to happen the way it did for the neighbor kids. If we were to have anything, we had to plan for it.

Mom purchased this old-time miniature adding machine to help her keep track of the groceries that we put in our cart so that we wouldn't be embarrassed at the checkout counter.

Each week, in those days before credit cards, my father gave my mother a certain amount of money with which to buy groceries, pay the bills, and run the household. On Saturday mornings, before he went to work at his second job, my brother and I went to the local grocery store with Mom to shop.

We walked the aisles while she went through her grocery list. She would ask us to go and get something off her list and put it in the cart. My brother and I would usually find something else we wanted, such as cookies or snacks, and we'd throw those into the cart too. I vividly remember getting to the checkout counter and my mother being told the total was more than she had. We had to go through everything and take the cookies, snacks, and other impulse purchases back to the aisles. Although that was embarrassing, it taught me that we could not just throw everything that we wanted in the basket. If we wanted cookies and snacks, we had to learn how to plan and budget for them.

Today, many people put what they cannot afford on a credit card and think that they'll figure it out later. In those days, it was humbling to realize how much we had to think about living within our means, especially when our means compared unfavorably to those around us.

This important early influence helped me to appreciate what I have and watch how I spend my money. It helped me to create a value system based on knowing how to think about money.

The Value of Hard Work

Although my mother had limited funds for groceries and household expenses, she had a great work ethic. She was a good baker, so she made Danish pastries, cookies, pies, and cakes. My brother and I went around to the neighbors, selling them. Our neighborhood was not big, but the other kids, who had more money than we did, teased us. Often I felt humiliated even though I wanted to help Mom in any way I could.

We did not get paid for selling the goods. At that time, the only reward was Mom's gratitude for a job well done. She didn't speak negatively about our dad, but she did let us know that we were helping her make ends meet. This made me feel like we were part of the process, and that feeling was rewarding in and of itself.

In those early years, my mechanically inclined Uncle Ray also taught me about the value of work. When I needed a bicycle, he took me to a yard sale and bought me a used bike. We sanded it, painted it, and got it in working order. Wow, I thought. With a little innovation, I could have a bike that was as good as new for a lot less.

The Value of Doing Things Right

Mom was the oldest of seven children. Her parents passed away within six months of each other when I was less than a year old. Several of her younger siblings had to move in and live with us for a few years after my grandparents died.

Because Dad worked two jobs, he wasn't around the house on a day-to-day basis for any length of time, so Mom became the disciplinarian. She taught us the value of doing things right. For example, if we were cutting the lawn, she instructed us to cut it in straight rows, so that it looked nice when it was done. If we were trimming the shrubs, we had to make sure they were all the same height. If we were sweeping out the garage, we had to do the entire job, right down to the corners, correctly.

Mom would come out to see how we were doing, and if we had hurried through a job or ignored part of a job, she'd say, "Do it again."

"But, Mom," I'd say. "Most of this is fine. We'll just do this part that's not quite right."

"Not good enough," she'd tell us. "You either do it right the first time, or you do it all over again."

One summer day, my brother and I were cutting the grass when we decided to play ball with the neighbor kids. In our eagerness to get away, we missed a few spots.

When we finished, we called Mom. "We're done," I said. "Going to play ball."

She checked our work, and I cringed as she discovered a few missed spots. "What about this and this?" she asked.

We ran over to our sloppy spots to fix them.

"No," she said. "You're going to cut the entire lawn again, and you're going to do the whole yard."

My brother groaned. "Mom," I insisted. "It's just these couple of spots."

"You know the rule," she replied. "Do it right or do it all over again." She made us cut the lawn in the opposite direction to make sure that we did the whole yard again. I'm sure she also knew she was teaching us a lesson we would not soon forget.

In high school, in addition to doing chores around the house, my brother and I were recruited to help Uncle Ray, who had a large yard with a wooden fence that needed to be repainted. It was my first paying job, and I was relieved when Uncle Ray made it clear that he wasn't too fussy and just wanted us to get the paint on. When we were about two-thirds through slapping paint on the fence, Mom came along to do an inspection and was less than happy with our performance. We protested.

"Uncle Ray just told us to slap this stuff on," I said.

"You know the rule," she said. "Do it right or do it again."

We had to go back and start at the beginning and redo the entire fence.

Back then, I was upset because we were just there to get it done. However, we weren't raised to just get it done. Years later, I came to appreciate the fact that Mom instilled a good work ethic in me and in my brother. This was particularly evident when I got a job on a small horse farm during high school. The owner, Waldo Brown, raised a handful of horses and raced them. He also owned a Buick and an Oldsmobile dealership in Pittsburgh. In the wintertime, I cleaned the stalls, and in the summertime, I baled the hay. I drove the tractor and creosoted all the fences to stop the horses chewing on them. Waldo was a great person and a harder worker, and he expected things to be done right. When it came to my work, he had no complaints.

Mom had instilled in me the values that hard work is important, doing it right is important, and paying attention to details is important. Those values have stuck with me through life and in business.

> Mom had instilled in me the values that hard work is important, doing it right is important, and paying attention to details is important.

The Value of Common Sense

Those early lessons teach us not just what we want for ourselves but what we don't want. For many years I couldn't understand how Dad could work so hard for his money and then gamble it away, denying himself and his family the things that money could have bought. Only when I was in high school did I learn that gambling is a sickness, like alcoholism or drug addiction. I do not believe that Dad understood the risks he was taking. Nevertheless, when I was growing up, he played the numbers and was always looking to make the big hit. He let greed get in the way of common sense.

I grew up knowing that I never wanted to risk the roof over my head the way he did. Although he was a hard worker and well intentioned, he made mistakes. Thankfully, I learned from those mistakes. Seeing his struggle taught me that you don't gamble what you can't afford to lose.

The Value of Listening

Because Dad worked two jobs, I did not get to spend a lot of time with him, so I often rode with him in the evening and on Saturdays as he drove to Pittsburgh to the furniture store where he worked his second job selling furniture. I did my homework at the furniture store while he worked. The two brothers who owned the store took my dad under their wings and treated him very well.

As the brothers and my Dad talked to various customers in their store, I listened. They showed customers different furniture pieces and answered their questions. When they made a sale, I asked how it happened. One of the brothers—his name was Morris, but he asked me to call him Uncle Joe—said, "The way they answer helps me understand what they're looking for and what they can afford."

From there, he could show them furniture and fabrics that met their needs. I was a naturally inquisitive child, perhaps because I was trying so hard to figure out how life worked and how I could create a stable future for myself. Uncle Joe and my Dad taught me a great deal about how to listen.

The Value of Giving Back

When we went to church on Sundays, my parents gave my brother and me a nickel or a dime to put in the offering basket because they believed it was important to give back to the church. My mother baked for the school or church bake sales to help them raise money. When we outgrew our clothes, we found someone to give them to or a place that took donations.

Today, I still believe in giving back to the church and the community. As I said in the introduction to this book, I believe there are givers and takers in this world. Some people who are in a financial position to help others fail to do so. I have never understood that. I was raised to believe that there are certain basic principles of life, and one of them is kindness and being a Good Samaritan. That stayed with me. I believe that when you give, somewhere along the line, it comes back tenfold. You may not know when or how, but it will come back to you.

I find it rewarding when I can do something to help improve an organization or an individual or the life of a family in some way. This became a core value in my financial planning profession. It is a way to give back by helping people improve their lives. My belief in giving is probably one reason financial planning and not sales attracted me to this profession in the first place.

> I find it rewarding when I can do something to help improve an organization or an individual or the life of a family in some way. This became a core value in my financial planning profession.

LESSONS FROM EARLY CAREER EXPERIENCES

While childhood brought its own rewards, challenges, and experiences that forged my value system from an early age, these values were further enhanced and broadened in my first career steps as a young adult. From working as a part-time bill collector while I was in college to selling insurance, I developed an understanding of how to think about people's challenges and their needs.

Lessons from Debt Collecting

I went to college in Columbus, Ohio, to study business finance. After my freshman year, I had a wife and a child, which meant that I had to both work and go to school full time. My first job was as a bill collector for a credit card company. My job was to call people who were behind on their payments and try to convince them that they should pay something on their debt. That experience taught me a great deal about people and about life.

Working as a debt collector quickly taught me that a lot of people run up debt and don't pay their bills on time. Given the lessons of my upbringing in budgeting and planning, this was a surprise. I met them, worked with them, and followed up to make sure that if they promised to pay, they paid. A lot of people promised to pay and did not. At nineteen years old, I realized there were many different kinds of people in the world when it came to managing money.

Bill collecting was challenging, but it was rewarding in the sense that I was recognized for being good at it. The company gave me some of the toughest people to collect from and challenged me to convince them to pay. I approached by first trying to understand them, why they made certain purchases, and why they were unable to pay. Because I was a good listener, I was able to convince many of them that paying their bill was the right thing to do and that they had an obligation to pay. In those days, it was possible to waive the interest charges on credit cards if they stuck to a payment plan, so I put a carrot out there, explaining that the company could be flexible in setting up a payment plan that factored in their income and expenses. I showed how they could have a surplus, and this surplus could go toward paying down a small amount of their debt. At the end of the day, that felt good to them because they made progress. In each case, the solution came from my listening to and trying to understand the individual who owed money and tailoring a solution to their needs.

I had no formal learning in this area, but it came naturally after hours watching Uncle Joe and Dad work in the furniture store and asking them questions that they answered in words I could understand. Often Dad and I talked about these ideas on our drive home from the store. I also related to these people who had made purchases on credit and now were forced to face the consequences of not being able to pay for them. I didn't feel superior to the people on the other end of the phone call. I had witnessed, at close range, what they were going through.

Lessons from Selling Insurance

In 1976, when I was twenty-five years old, I started to work in the insurance industry, selling life insurance, disability insurance, and health insurance. This was another eye-opening experience.

Working as an insurance agent meant effectively working alone as a self-employed individual licensed through an agency. The company provided a base salary for a short period of time and some training for new hires to get started. From there, I had to build up a client list and become proficient at sales. After a certain period, the base salary went away, and, as an insurance agent, I was on my own.

In those days, we made cold calls. We got on the phone and dialed numbers. It was all a numbers game. If I dialed one hundred people, I would probably talk to forty. A third of those might say yes to a meeting, and about three of those would end up buying a policy. It was hard work.

The insurance company I worked for had a system that they called needs analysis. This involved trying to identify how much insurance somebody needed based on their goals and objectives. This meant that, aside from learning selling and marketing techniques, I also had to gather information that allowed me to say, "Based on what you've told me, here's what you're trying to do. If something were to happen to you and you didn't have an income stream coming in or you passed away, your family would be left in this position. To avoid this, here's how much insurance you need."

In the insurance business, questions have to be answered in order to know how much income someone has and how they spend it. From these questions, it is possible to quickly see who is living beyond their means.

My experience as a bill collector helped me categorize my potential customers. When prospecting, I could easily determine which ones had potential and which ones were too far in debt to take on one more expense. Some people were just bad money managers. They had income and expenses, but they were living for today and putting off worrying about tomorrow.

When I started asking questions, I saw some red flags in terms of what people were doing right and wrong. This gave me a perspective about how to help them. I could help them think a little differently about how they spent money and prioritize properly in terms of short-, intermediate-, and long-term goals. I realized that if I could help people identify their goals and their objectives, I could help them identify how to get there. When people can see the light at the end of that tunnel, it is possible to help them go down that path. I believed that then, and I know it now for a fact.

I learned early that I had a knack for looking at complex issues from thirty thousand feet in the air and making them simple and straightforward so that people could understand them. People often procrastinate because something seems too complex. However, as with Uncle Joe explaining sales to me, when someone is able to understand, they are able to take positive action.

It does not follow that because a person has great skills in one area of their life, they are good at managing assets and finances and/or evaluating risk. If a car breaks down, the owner can choose to fix it themself or take it to a professional. If a person has a toothache, they can try to extract it or go to a dentist. In all these scenarios, including financial planning, a professional can help people fix the problem or get to the bottom line.

TAKEAWAY

→ Growing up when money was tight was a great teacher about what I wanted and what I did not want out of life. We learned to manage through hard work and budgeting.

→ By my midtwenties, I learned how hard it is for some people to live within their means and manage their money. Asking a lot of questions and gathering a lot of information made it possible for me to help them, first with insurance products and later as a financial planner. From working with people to managing money, whether that be repaying debt, managing income and expenses, or planning for the future, I learned what questions to ask to get them and keep them on track. The more I learned about customers, the more I could help them turn the corner to become better money managers and accumulate enough money to draw a line in the sand and decide if they wanted to continue working.

→ My formative years taught me many core values, among them proper planning, hard work, doing it right the first time, common sense, listening, and giving back. But the one that stands out most is an ongoing desire to help people. From selling pastries for my mother to working with Uncle Joe and Waldo Brown, I learned I felt best about myself when I was helping people. As I moved into my career, this transformed into helping people clarify and attain their financial and lifestyle goals and objectives, which we will look at in more detail next.

CHAPTER 4

Building a Corporate Vision

Selling insurance had limited potential when it came to helping people beyond assessing their insurance needs and selling them a product. People needed real help when it came to investments, retirement, estate planning, and tax planning. In the late 1970s, a new branch of study was emerging in the financial world—financial planning. The College for Financial Planning in Denver, Colorado, had a series of five self-study courses that could be taken over two years and promised to offer skills and training for those who wanted to help others. In 1980, I started to take the courses. Once you completed a self-study course, you could sit for a proctored exam at one of four universities in the US. One was The Ohio State University. After two years of study, with the requisite industry experience under my belt, I earned my certification as a CFP® in 1982.

The real need that had to be met did not involve making suggestions or recommendations to people based on how much money I could make in fees and commissions. The way to effectively help was trying to understand a particular individual's financial circumstances, their goals and objectives, their concerns, how they managed money, and where they stood taxwise.

The first and most basic question in every meeting with every client was personal to me. My thought was this: With my knowledge and expertise, if I were sitting in your shoes, what kind of planning would I do?

This was the method by which Chornyak & Associates gave advice, and it proved to be very successful.

TAILORING A VISION OF INVESTMENT

Typically, our clients are referred to us by either an existing client or an attorney or CPA who is familiar with our firm. At Chornyak & Associates, before meeting potential clients face to face, we have a telephone conversation. We use this as an opportunity to introduce the company and find out relevant information about the potential client. We ask what prompted them to call. Often it's because they received an inheritance, or they are unhappy with their existing advisor, or they lost their job, or they are getting a divorce.

In the initial face-to-face meeting that follows, our goal is to get a good idea of who they are. That includes what they are trying to accomplish and what their financial situation looks like. That way, we can tell them if we are a good fit, in which areas they need help, and in which areas we believe we can help. Because their responses might prompt other questions, listening actively—a skill every good financial planner must develop—is essential.

Therefore, we ask them to prepare for our meeting by bringing in recent statements from any type of accounts that they have, which may be a bank account, a money market account, an investment account, a retirement account, a 401(k) account, and/or an IRA. We ask them to bring recent statements from any debts that they have, such as their mortgage, home equity line of credit, car loans or car leases, credit card debt, and any other outstanding obligations. We also ask them to bring in paycheck stubs to assess their income and their withholding and two years' tax returns along with supporting documents and any other pertinent documents, such as life insurance policies, car insurance, homeowners insurance, umbrella policies, wills and trust documents, any employment agreements that they may have, copies of the deeds to their real estate, copies of titles to their car or cars, and recent social security statements.

These documents allow us to start to paint a picture of their financial life. From there, we can assess their lifestyle and how well versed they are in their finances. We ask why they have certain debts or investments, what they like or dislike about these investments, what they want, and what keeps them up at night.

Most important, we ask, "If we were sitting at this table three years from now reflecting back on the last three years, what needs to change in your life both professionally and personally in order for you to feel good about your progress?"

Once we analyze this data, we formulate a financial plan that identifies where they are today, where they need to go, and the road map they need to get there.

Here's what we usually find.

The client isn't properly diversified. They often have a high concentration of stock in the companies they've worked for, or the bulk of the money in their retirement account is in that company's stock or an aggressive mix of passively managed index funds. This is a mistake we'll look at in more detail later in the book.

The client is taking a shotgun approach. They have a little bit invested in lots of different places: some good, some mediocre, and some really bad. Because they don't know what's good or what's bad, they reason, "If I put a little bit in here, and a little bit in here, I'll get the averages." They don't have the expertise to sort through the various choices, so they take a broad brush and put a little bit in a lot of places.

The client has failed to factor in fees. They do not realize that in many instances, they are spending 2 percent to 2½ percent a year in fees, charges, and expenses for advice. That's quite a handicap for an investor trying to accumulate money for long-term retirement. The total cost of advice should be approximately 1 percent or less on an annual basis. People often fail to see the hidden costs that exist in an investment in addition to the advisor's fee. These costs include the underlying expenses embedded in mutual funds. In other words, if the total investment cost (advisory fees plus the internal costs of the underlying investments) is high, it eats into the net long-term rate of return that the investor receives.

COMPONENTS OF AN INVESTMENT VISION

Money magazine, the *Wall Street Journal, Investor's Business Daily*, and many industry publications that exist alongside the news media and advertising industry focus on rate of return, which means this is where most people look when they turn to investing. However, as I mentioned previously, looking at rate of return in a vacuum is a huge mistake because it fails to look at several factors, including how much risk is being taken for that return, how well the portfolio is managed, who is managing it, or whether it is diversified.

If one investment is generating 8 percent and another investment is generating 12 percent, the obvious pick is 12 percent. However, there is more often than not significantly higher risk associated with that 12 percent rate of return. Higher return almost always equates to higher risk. This is why it is better to think of rate of return like a paycheck. A person goes to work, puts in the time, works for a week or two weeks, and gets a reward at the end of that time period, which is a paycheck. This is the rate of return for a job well done.

If you invest properly, this mindset will serve you well. You need to look ahead. Before we recommend a portfolio of mutual funds to a client, we first look at how well a fund's money is invested and whether the goals and objectives of that fund are the same as they were three, five, or ten years ago. Goals can shift, and the historic rate of return might not be the same today as it was yesterday. A surprising number of mutual fund investments today have dramatically changed their stripes over the years. As a result, the approach we take for our clients involves understanding how a fund invests the money, historically and today, and whether this has been consistent over time. This approach has worked well for us for more than thirty-five years.

The next questions we ask before investing a client's money in a fund are who is managing it and how long have they been at the helm. A fund can have the same goals and objectives, but if the management team today is different than it was three years ago, that historic rate of return is not indicative of the current portfolio management. It is best to think of investing like a work of art rather than painting by the numbers. Anyone can buy a kit that maps out all the variables and produce a painting, but compared to the work of an artist, the result of a paint-by-numbers kit would be markedly different. In the same way, the fund manager's talent, training, and experience will also make a big difference.

Another key factor in our investment vision is diversification. We look at a fund's diversification before recommending it to a client. We look at what kind of stocks and bonds it uses because this directly relates to how much risk is involved.

Rate of return by itself doesn't give people a clear understanding of how money is being invested, where, or by whom, which is why we recommend making rate of return the last thing that is looked at, not the starting place in making investment decisions.

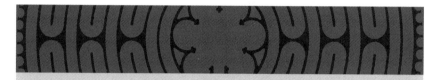

When evaluating a particular mutual fund, you should ask the following questions:

1. What are the goals or objectives of the mutual fund?

    a. Stocks?

    b. Bonds?

    c. Both?

2. Who is managing the mutual fund, and how long have they been managing the money?

3. How are they diversifying the portfolio?

    a. By industry?

    b. By company?

    c. Geographically?

4. Finally, what has the long-term rate of return been over a full market cycle adjusted for risk and expenses?

BUILDING A VISIONARY TEAM

At Chornyak & Associates, we make it a point to hire people who have an innate inquisitiveness, common sense, and the ability to learn. Each team member needs to think and analyze, not always on their own but as part of our team. This allows us to keep an overall corporate vision that's based on listening, asking questions, gathering lots of information, and drawing on the decades of real-life experience possessed within the walls of our company to do what's best for our clients' bank accounts, not our own. Because we listen, we are good at helping clients develop long-term goals and objectives and a plan to attain them. Our clients trust us because they know we believe in doing what's in their best interest.

We recently had a longtime employee who retired after eighteen years. Clients sent her personal notes, thanking her for all the years of service and the help she provided to them. They commented on how she walked the extra mile to get things done and how she followed up to make things easier for them. There were many notes saying, "We're going to miss you" and "You were our go-to person." This is what we expect of everyone inside our organization. We want every client's experience to be one where he or she knows we walked the extra mile.

We know that clients can go anywhere to purchase an investment. In this day and age, technology means they can do it themselves. Therefore, we know that to differentiate ourselves, we need to provide exemplary service and offer advice based on a higher level of quality and

> We know that to differentiate ourselves, we need to provide exemplary service and offer advice based on a higher level of quality and objectivity.

objectivity. This means giving advice based on what clients need to know, not necessarily what they want to hear.

A husband and wife came to us recently who hadn't updated their estate plan because, like many people, they weren't quite sure what to do. When we reviewed their financial affairs, we realized that they had accounts everywhere. Their financial situation was so complex that they couldn't understand what to do with it. The clients had been procrastinating because they didn't know how to move forward. Their advisor of fifteen years had died a number of years ago, and they hadn't made any changes since then. They were referred to us by a trusted friend, and we went through our process, meeting with them and assessing their finances, goals, desires, and concerns. We shared our concerns about their estate plan, their investment mix, and their retirement. From there, we consolidated their myriad accounts, coordinated a meeting with a local estate planning attorney, discussed how they could take advantage of changes in tax laws, and ultimately got them on the path toward understanding their goals and accomplishing them.

People procrastinate when they don't know what to do, which is why a core value at our firm is to start by asking what they want to accomplish and then ask why they want to accomplish it. This gives us a sense of their vision. Once we have that, we can get to work and develop a plan on how to get everything done.

A VISION FOR GIVING

As I mentioned earlier, an important part of our corporate vision (and my personal vision) is giving back. In the early years, it was more informal than it is now. We will look at this in more detail later in the book, but from the beginning, it was important that our firm give back in some way, including giving back to the community monetarily, giving back in terms of time, and giving back by helping people in need who might not be able to afford our services.

Many people work hard but need a helping hand. From the beginning, giving back was ingrained in our corporate culture. For example, we believe in local broadcasting and have been supporting and sponsoring the local National Public Radio station for more than twenty years. We give to the local Boy Scouts by sponsoring their annual programs, and we give to the local arts council to support local community efforts. We support the Arthritis Foundation and the Make-a-Wish Foundation. Joe Chornyak Jr. is very active in Pelotonia, which raises funds for innovative cancer research at The Ohio State University Comprehensive Cancer Center, so we provide matching dollars.

DETERMINING QUALITY

When we sit down with a client and ask them where they want to go, we are really asking them to envision the quality of life they want in the future.

Before they decide where they want to go, they need to figure out where they are and how they got there.

TAKEAWAY

The most fundamental philosophy at Chornyak & Associates is to always treat others as you want to be treated. For the last forty years, it has been an integral part of our culture to offer advice only after obtaining a clear understanding of where the client stands taxwise, their risk temperament, what they want to accomplish, and why. From there, we can offer the honest advice of "if I were in your shoes, these are the things I would do."

At the end of the day, clients should be able to reach a level of financial success whereby they can draw a line in the sand and have choices—for example, working past retirement age because they want to, not because they have to. To do this, a good financial advisor should tell them what they need to know, not what they want to hear, and from there, involve them in a logical and objectives-based decision-making process that focuses on the end result—a long-term bulletproof investment portfolio—and not on the starting point—rate of return.

CHAPTER 5

How to Think about Quality of Life

Part of the reason we gather so much information is because we cannot tell somebody what they need to do, where they need to go, or how they are going to get there until we have a clear understanding of where they are today, how they got where they are today, and what they like or dislike about where they are today. To this end, it's important to break down and add up expenses and identify what is superfluous spending.

Everyone, rich and poor, spends money based on needs and wants. Needs are things that they can't do without, such as mortgage payments or rent, utilities, and phone bills. We suggest to people that they put an *X* by the things on their list that aren't necessary. This allows them to separate how they are spending money into two categories: needs and wants. They can see what they absolutely cannot change and what they can. This is often an aha moment. They come to the realization that the morning latte at the local coffee shop is turning into a one-hundred-dollar-a-month expense, and they can then decide if that is a need or a want.

When you take a look at your cash flow by what is coming in versus what's going out, you gain some perspective on your financial picture and can decide what you like and dislike about it. In other words, you can see how your financial picture contributes to or detracts from your quality of life. You can assess your life to see what caused you to get where you are, to spend how you do, and to accumulate what you own. Once you see this picture, you can start to make decisions to lead the life you want. You can also decide what you like enough in your life and what you do not, what will help you get to where you want to be and what will not, what burdens mean you will have to work beyond the age at which you want to retire, and what will allow you to leave a legacy.

Once you identify what you do not like, you can start making changes. As mentioned previously, a common question in my strategic coaching program is: If you and I were sitting here three years from today and reflecting back over the last three years, what would need to happen both personally and professionally for you to feel good about your progress? This is a thought-provoking question. It makes people think about the choices that enhance or detract from the quality of their lives.

Once a client has painted this picture of the life they desire, the purpose of the financial planner is to then help them create the road map that will get them from *A*, where they are today, to *B*, where they want to be in the future. At our firm, as the advisor, we try to keep them on track by making them accountable so that they don't give in to impulse *wants* at the expense of long-term *needs*.

QUALITY-OF-LIFE CHECKUP

Having a periodic checkup and being accountable to somebody is like having an annual physical, or a six-month dental cleaning and exam. Sometimes a dentist will identify that the patient has a cavity or a cracked tooth. This makes the patient accountable for doing the work to take care of their teeth. If they haven't been toeing the line in terms of eating habits, their cholesterol may be high, and the doctor will hold them accountable for making adjustments. Financial affairs are no different.

A financial planner can walk you through the steps that most people aren't disciplined enough to do on their own. Much like traveling, more will be accomplished with a tour guide than wandering about alone.

Looking to the future, an advisor can help a client establish how much money is needed for retirement or how much they need to leave a legacy, if that is a goal. Clients need a guide to help them avoid paying excess taxes or avoid missing a tax reduction. Those who are uncertain about the structure of their portfolio or their rate of return, those who have accumulated a nest egg and do not want the government to take a chunk of it, those who lie awake at night wondering if they are set up for a fall, need an advisor to help remove this stress to improve their quality of life, now and in the future.

Quality of life can only improve with regular checkups with a trusted financial professional, who will make sure the client's choices support a good quality of life, such as being properly diversified, thinking the right way about money, whether goals are set and being reassessed, or whether they are making decisions that won't cause tax penalties. We will discuss these concerns in later chapters.

IT'S WHO, NOT HOW

What often prevents people from having the quality of life they desire is their lack of belief that it is possible. Too many times, people say, "I don't know how I'm ever going to be able to retire, and so I'm probably going to work for the rest of my life." They often get hung up on questions such as: How are we going to do it? Do we have enough accumulated in money market accounts, or checking accounts, or CDs? Do we buy mutual funds, or index funds, or individual stocks, or annuities? People also get hung up on taxes and often let the tax decision overshadow the right investment decision.

> What often prevents people from having the quality of life they desire is their lack of belief that it is possible.

Ultimately, people can worry about all of these questions so much that they end up believing they can never attain the quality of life they want.

Our response is, "Let's figure out where you are today and what you're doing, and let's try to identify how you can retire when you want to." From there, we do our analysis and give them a retirement projection looking into the future under conservative assumptions. We paint a future projection that shows them what retirement looks like between social security, retirement benefits, and income from other assets they have accumulated.

More often than not, people are surprised to see that they can actually get to a place that had seemed unattainable. Most are so busy just living day to day that they do not have time to research the answer to how to manage their money and thus their quality of life. Instead of asking, "How can I do this?" they should be asking, "Who can help me figure out how to do this?"

The solution is out there, and it just requires finding who can help them set and accomplish their goals. In that way, future security can be mapped out, and a person's present life isn't marred by stress and worry.

HOW TO THINK ABOUT QUALITY

Life is a series of trade-offs. We do not know whether we are going to be alive tomorrow, but we need to find a balance between living for today and planning for tomorrow.

Occasionally, people unknowingly pass that line in the sand where they have enough money to do what they want. They continue to deal with the stress of work and worry about whether their portfolio is structured properly to retire, while in fact, they do not have to be in the office or on the road seven days a week at all.

Knowing when that line in the sand has been crossed helps people to stop worrying and start planning. Identifying when the means to have the desired quality of life has been attained is important. When people realize they have reached that point, they can relax. They can enjoy life more. They can start counting down to their retirement day because they know it is coming. They can see the light at the end of the tunnel for a bigger, better future. This often prompts them to start thinking about their health and diet because they have the time and space to do so. Thus, in many ways, quality of life can improve.

Another factor in determining quality of life is personal satisfaction, feeling good, and helping people in need. Some people reach a place where their passion is giving back to the community, and having a new income stream after retirement allows them to do this. People often find time to prepare holiday dinners for the needy or lonely or volunteer at a nonprofit organization. There is a great deal of satisfaction to be had in sharing and giving.

TAKEAWAY

Questions about retirement include the following: What do I want to do? Where do I like to travel? Do I want to move to a milder climate? Do I want to take my children or grandchildren on an annual trip? Could I be more involved in the church or a nonprofit organization? Could I go back to school, learn a different trade, or become more knowledgeable about wines or gardening or sewing?

Asking these questions helps a person to frame what quality of life means to them. It is subjective and different for everyone. Nobody can do everything; everyone has limitations and ranges, but thinking about quality of life in retirement can also help define long-term goals. Knowing where a person wants to be tomorrow can help keep them on track today.

Thinking about quality of life relates to thinking about goals. Many people fear that they will never have the life they want. They think they'll have to work until the bitter end, but that's not the case. Knowing what they want from life and what they want to achieve just requires planning. Once you determine the life you want, you can devise a financial road map to get there by the choices and decisions you make today. This reduces stress and fear of the future.

The first step in manifesting this kind of quality of life comes from learning to think properly about money, which we will now examine.

CHAPTER 6

How to Think about Money

On a flight from Dallas a year ago, a man who had been an engineer in the military explained to me that he had gone to a major investment firm for financial planning help and was told he was not big enough for them. This is a common story. All too often, people who want to start investing money or planning for retirement go to a "financial advisor," who is often an investment advisor or stockbroker trying to peddle a product and who tells them they do not have enough investment money to work with their firm. The individual investor then often tries to manage his or her financial affairs without the expertise even to set up a college fund, never mind plan for retirement. Like many individual investors, this engineer was thinking about saving for retirement, which is an admirable goal, but his priorities were wrong. He had credit card debt and student loans, yet he was still trying to put money into a 401(k) and other investments. He was putting the cart before the horse. In other words, he was thinking the wrong way about money.

This chapter will focus on the common mistakes people make when thinking about money. We'll look at the right way to think about it as well. And we'll examine different types of money—that is, short-, medium-, and long-term money and how that relates to investing. You'll learn to determine how much of each should be held in reserve or invested. Think of this chapter as your investment road map as you learn how to think about money and the hows and whys of investing.

DETERMINING YOUR OVERALL FINANCIAL PICTURE

The first step in any financial plan involves getting a handle on the investor's overall financial picture. First comes your debt load.

The engineer I met on the flight hadn't looked at all his assets and liabilities, the interest he was paying on outstanding debts, and the interest he was receiving on other accounts. This is a common mistake. People have credit card debt with double-digit interest rates, which is non-tax-deductible. They have car loans at a high interest rate, which is also not tax deductible. These debts impede their progress, but they do not realize this because they've been looking at things in buckets and saying, "Okay, this is my bucket for debt, and I make monthly payments on this. This is my bucket for savings, and I put in X amount per month."

It's important to understand that when you have credit card debt with interest rates anywhere between 12.9 percent and 21.9 percent that the interest you are paying is not tax deductible. Furthermore, it's nearly impossible for you to have a well-diversified investment portfolio that will have an annual after-tax rate of return that is higher than what you're paying to the credit card companies.

The first step therefore is to devise a plan to get debt free. This might involve consolidating debt into a low-interest home equity line of credit or another debt-management plan. It should definitely involve putting as much money as possible toward the highest interest-rate debt first and paying that off as soon as possible. This effectively gives you a higher rate of return in the long run because it eliminates high-interest debt that is impeding your long-term progress. This is common sense. With very few exceptions, an investment will never generate the rate of return that a bank is charging in credit card interest or on a car loan.

You need to decide where your money will serve you best. When you evaluate your 401(k) contribution, you should also consider these three factors:

- Employer matching contribution

- Investment return

- Tax savings

Next you should target high-rate debt.

If you are paying interest on debt, in many cases, it is better to reduce your 401(k) contributions and take some of that money to wipe out your debt over a period of months in order to get financially healthy. Very often, people put 10 percent or 15 percent of their paycheck away in a 401(k) plan at their company for retirement. Sometimes the company does not provide a match, or it only matches the first 6 percent. Yet people believe this is still a good decision. People tend to think in buckets, which does not help their investment strategy. They

> If you are paying interest on debt, in many cases, it is better to reduce your 401(k) contributions and take some of that money to wipe out your debt over a period of months in order to get financially healthy.

think they are doing the right thing by putting 10 percent or 15 percent of their paycheck into a 401(k) when, in reality, they need to reduce their 401(k) contributions temporarily, even though that will involve paying taxes on more wages, to pay off the debt that hurts more in the long run.

Before moving forward, it is important to clean up past sins. Once you have eliminated your high-interest debt, you can start accumulating some savings. Let's turn our attention to the different types of money that every investor needs.

DIFFERENT TYPES OF MONEY

To create a financial plan that continues to generate a paycheck after the breadwinner stops working, you must understand the difference between short-term, intermediate-term, and long-term money. No matter what the stage of life, before thinking about long-term investing, you must understand the difference between true investment money and money that is in reserve and allows you to sleep at night when markets are volatile.

Short-Term Money

Short-term money is an emergency reserve. It could be the money in a checking, savings, or money market account, some of which you spend during the month. It could even be money that you have buried in a tin can in your backyard or under a mattress. Regardless of where you keep it, this is your cash reserve, and it's not investment money.

To determine short-term money needs, you must examine and understand your cash-flow needs and spending habits. Spending patterns over the previous few months will paint this picture. Going through your expenses for several months will show you how much you need, on a monthly basis, to maintain your current living standards. You'll see how much you're spending daily, weekly, and monthly on the mortgage payment, car lease payment, utilities, cell phone, and everyday expenses like groceries. That will tell you what you need monthly to maintain your current living standard, which is also the basis for determining the amount you should hold in short-term or liquid money, so that you'll have enough for the next three to six months in the event of a job loss or disability.

If, for example, you need $5,000 a month, then it is important that you have $15,000–$30,000 in reserve for emergencies before you need to dip into your long-term investment money. Until you have this fund in place, you should not be thinking about investing long term because doing so will make you vulnerable to the market. You might even have to pull that money from long-term investments when the market is down. We'll discuss this in more detail later in this chapter.

If you're married, you may need closer to three months of cash in reserve if one of you is still earning an income. Having two sources of income can allow you to adjust how much you need to keep short term.

Intermediate-Term Money

Intermediate-term money is cash you keep in reserve to cover the expenses I mentioned previously for another twelve to eighteen months. This could be in CDs with staggered maturities, in short-term bonds, or in a short-term bond mutual fund that is not affected by the stock market. These do not generate the highest rate of return; however, they are a backup so that if the market takes a downturn, you still have a source to draw from once your short-term money is exhausted. In other words, intermediate-term money helps you ride out the storm. This means that, in the event of a job loss or an unanticipated major expense, you have money in an investment vehicle that is earning a small rate of return without being at risk in the stock market.

Long-Term Money

Long-term money can be tied up for anywhere from two to ten years plus. This is the money that can weather the storm of the stock market's volatility. If the market takes a downturn, this money can stay there until there's an upswing. If short-term money is a forty-yard sprint, long-term money is a marathon.

The most common long-term goal I see among individual investors is having enough money to retire. Other goals include setting aside enough money to help children or grandchildren go to college. Some people have the goal of changing their profession down the road or pursuing their passions, which could be traveling or learning a new skill. Some people want a second home. Others dream of embarking on a philanthropic project to give back to their church, charity, or community.

Goals help us stay focused on accumulating and saving because they give us a purpose. Goals also help us delay gratification in a world where we have been conditioned to want everything now. So you say to yourself, "I'm not going to buy that sporty red Porsche because it is more important to me to tuck that money away, because my long-term goal is to spend my winters traveling to warmer climates."

Like running a marathon, long-term goals require planning and preparation. In the financial world, that planning means thinking about money in terms of the short term, medium term, and long term. Short-term and intermediate-term planning creates a safety net that allows an investor's long-term money to grow over the long haul since long-term investments, by their very nature, have more risk.

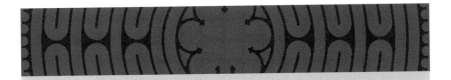

3 TYPES OF MONEY

1. Short-term: minimum of three to six months

    - Checking account

    - Savings account

    - Money market account

2. Intermediate-term: twelve to eighteen months

    - CDs

    - Short-term bonds

3. Long-term

    - Stock mutual funds

    - Bond mutual funds

    - Real estate

    - Collectibles

The basic principle of investing is a phrase you've probably heard dozens of times: "Buy low, sell high." Too often, people take all their money and invest it in the market because it is going up. Then the market drops, or the furnace breaks, or they lose their job, and these investors have to sell at a loss because they did not plan properly. Other people end up selling low when emergency situations arise. Setting goals means knowing what needs to be in reserve versus what can be invested, and where.

In addition to investment goals, you should set a retirement goal, or at least a goal of having enough money to be able to retire comfortably. That includes looking at what you've accumulated, including any company pension and social security. It is also important for you to look at what you are currently doing in terms of spending, saving, and investing. Sometimes those amounts will be aligned; sometimes you will need to invest more.

WHAT *NOT* TO DO: GIVE UP

Suppose you do everything I've suggested. You look at what's coming in, what's going out, and when. Then you realize you're not tucking away nearly enough. "How much more do I need?" you ask yourself. "Another $2,000 a month?" Then you throw up your hands and say, "I'm never going to get there."

Don't do this. You will get there. Furthermore, you have taken the first important step to do just that. You have figured out how much you need. Next you need a strategy, and that means incremental steps.

WHAT *TO* DO: INCREMENTAL STEPS

Create a time frame into which a goal can be broken down into shorter and more attainable increments. For example, if you want to lose twenty pounds, you don't give up because you're overwhelmed by that number. Instead, you spread that goal over six months. You can lose three pounds a month or less than a pound a week, right? This short-term goal helps you stay on track to ultimately reach your long-term goal. The key is incremental steps. Investment goals are exactly the same.

Do what can be done today. If that's only one hundred dollars a month, do it. Next year, you may get a pay increase that will allow you to put away a little more. A year after that, something else, such as a bonus or the receipt of stock options may appear. In this way, your retirement fund will gradually build. If these additional options become available, you should add them to what you're regularly putting away. Then your path to the ultimate goal will become one of progression rather than an all-or-nothing proposition. Progress is the key.

THE HOW AND WHO OF INVESTING

When many of us think about money, we often think about rate of return first. While rate of return is important, in my opinion, it should be the last thing that we look at. The most important first step is this: How is my money invested, and am I properly diversified? Instead of thinking about investing in individual stocks and bonds, you must think about investing in a variety of mutual funds. Remember, mutual funds have researchers, analysts, portfolio managers, and even forensic accountants who do nothing but look at and visit various companies, evaluate them, and build portfolios.

> The most important first step is this: How is my money invested, and am I properly diversified?

It is important that you think about how a fund invests its money. Does it buy stocks, bonds, or both? If the managers are buying stocks, are they buying stocks of large companies, medium-sized companies, small companies, or all of the above? Are they buying the stocks of companies that are headquartered in the United States or in other parts of the world? This is important because different parts of the world function differently. Sometimes the foreign markets do better than the US markets and vice versa. Therefore, it is important to be diversified globally, including in emerging markets.

How Is the Money Invested?

If a fund is invested in stocks, how it is invested matters. Are these stocks in pure growth companies that take all their profits and plow them back into the company to grow, or do they take some of their profits and pay them out to their shareholders in the form of dividends? Historically, companies that pay dividends tend to be more conservative than companies that do not. You need a cross section of both.

Many investors fail to examine whether the fund is investing the same way it was three, five, or ten years ago. If a mutual fund changed its investment approach and is investing differently today than it was five years ago, the historic rate of return is meaningless. When the kinds of companies and number of holdings change significantly, the fund becomes a different investment vehicle than it once was. It does not invest money today the same way it did in the past, which means it will probably be generating a different rate of return than it did in the past.

Who is managing the funds?

This is the next big question before you even think about rate of return. Professional management makes a big difference to the performance of a fund. Ten different portfolio managers will approach the portfolios in ten different ways. Therefore, it is important for you to ask the following:

- Is it managed by a single manager or a team of managers?

- How long have they been managing money in general and this fund in particular? If they have not been managing that mutual fund very long, then the historic track record becomes meaningless because the manager today is not the one who created the historic rate of return in the past.

- Do the managers of the fund have significant amounts of their own personal money invested in the mutual funds they manage? Do they have skin in the game? Annual filings with the SEC provide this information. Fund managers should have at least $1 million of their own money invested in the fund under management. Obviously, they have a vested interest in how the money is managed because their own money is at stake.

Studies have shown that some of the best performing mutual funds over ten-year rolling periods are those (1) where the current management has significant amounts of their own money invested in the funds under management; (2) where the current management has been managing that fund for at least one full market cycle, if not two or three; and (3) where the internal fund expenses are less than 1 percent annually.

Once an investor has either worked with a financial planner who has a philosophy of the how and the who of investing or has done the legwork personally, the next important issue when it comes to thinking about money involves common sense investing.

COMMON SENSE INVESTING

Investors often let their emotions drive investment decisions. As mentioned before, many individual investors invest their long-term money in stocks and mutual funds when they are doing well and sell them when they drop. Too many people want to get in when the markets are at an all-time high and get out when they are down 10 percent or 15 percent. In other words, contrary to the maxim, "Buy low, sell high," most investors buy high and sell low. Others hang on to their investments because they won't sell until they can get back what they paid for them. Others do not sell because they might have to take a loss or because they do not want to pay capital gains tax. None of these factors should be driving your decision. Rather than decide to hold on to a stock, bond, or mutual fund based on what you paid for it, you should ask yourself one question: Is this a good long-term investment today compared to other opportunities in the marketplace?

Riding Out the Market Cycle

The market goes through cycles. Over some time periods it is up, and over others it is down. And there are ups and downs within these cycles too. Historically, sometime during the calendar year, the stock market is typically down 5 percent to 7 percent with rare exceptions. On average, almost every three years, the market is down at least 10 percent to 15 percent. This means that 90–95 percent of the time, markets are down some time during the year and can be down 5 percent, 10 percent, 15 percent, or more. That said, since 1980, the stock market has actually ended the calendar year in positive territory approximately 75 percent of the time! In other words, markets are volatile in most calendar years, and no one knows when and to what extent this volatility will happen. What we do know is that the downturn is temporary, and it will end.

Downswings, even major ones like the rapid drop we experienced in 2020, should not be the time to panic about your long-term investments. As long as you have adequate short-term and intermediate-term money in reserve, you can ride through the storm. The key is how you think about long-term money and long-term investments.

A number of studies over the last twenty years have shown an average return on investment in the stock market of 9 percent or

10 percent. The average investor, however, earned about half that because they got in high and got out low. This is not investing; it is trading. A true investor needs to look at the long haul, not the short haul. This will help keep you from going into panic mode. When markets are down, you need to sit back and tell yourself (and anyone else who questions you), "This is a normal part of the investment cycle of the markets."

In the US and in most developed countries, about 70 percent of the economy is based on consumption, especially on essentials: toilet paper, laundry detergent, a visit to the dentist, toothpaste, household repairs, carpeting, refrigerators, gas for the car, new tires, electricity. Water will be drunk, and food will be eaten. Tires will wear out; grass will grow. Companies make these products, grow food, and provide these services, which means economies will bounce back. All you need is patience and an adequate cash reserve.

Commonsense Diversification

Once people think the right way about money, they know that long-term investments are not gambling. They are there for the marathon. To finish the marathon, you must be diversified and not let greed get in the way of common sense. This can be trickier than it seems. People have a difficult time separating their emotions and the amount of risk that they are taking because they look at rate of return in a vacuum without realizing how much risk they are taking.

A mutual fund could have gone up 50 percent last year, but the reason for this is increased risk. Then you have to ask yourself, "Is the risk worth it?" Except in rare cases, the answer is usually no. Reward for above-average risk is not usually enough to justify that risk.

For instance, if a driver has to travel 120 miles to get from one city to another, and the speed limit is 60 miles per hour, he will get there in two hours. If he drives at 100 miles per hour, he will get there twenty minutes early. Is this really worth the risk? Better to be the tortoise than the hare in this case. Finish the race. Be boring. Be slow and methodical. Don't be the jackrabbit with wild swings and wrecks along the way. Long-term money is about accumulating wealth for a lifetime. Investing for a lifetime is paced. It is steady. It is disciplined. It is unemotional, and it is broadly diversified. Always remember—it's a marathon!

Can you be too diversified?

Yes, you can. A couple of years ago, we began working with a new client who had no debt other than a low-interest-rate mortgage and who was saving money regularly. He and his wife were a couple of modest means who, over a period of years, amassed a net worth of more than $3 million. They lived in a modest home, drove modest vehicles, and lived frugally. They were cautious about how they spent money and spread their investments across many active and passive mutual funds, thinking that would mean they could never get hurt too badly.

Unfortunately, they put their money in too many places. He would pick up a *Money* magazine, read some article about another mutual fund, and buy into that. By the time they came to us, they had accounts everywhere. They did not know whether those investments were good or bad, so they just held them. All told, they had money in more than seventy different mutual funds. Some were doing fine, but some were awful. About 25 percent of their money was in cash because they had reached a point where they didn't know what else to do with their money. One look at their investments, and we knew they could have been doing much better.

In addition to their overly diversified portfolio, their investments were not titled properly for estate planning purposes, and their wills were out of date. They had no financial or medical power of attorney in place. They were intelligent people, but they never turned the corner on getting their financial house in order.

We took their seventy-plus holdings and consolidated them into fourteen actively managed mutual funds with fourteen teams of managers and gave them a more conservative well-diversified portfolio. We sat with an estate planning attorney to update their estate plan. We aligned the beneficiaries on their life insurance policies with their estate plan. We also aligned the beneficiaries on their 401(k)s and their trusts. We made sure that all of their accounts, including bank accounts and the deed to their home, had a transfer-on-death (TOD) provision to minimize whatever needed to go into probate.

Just as important, we also did some retirement projections to show them that they had already accumulated enough money to draw the line in the sand and decide, from that day forward, if they continued working, it was because they wanted to, not because they needed to. Even if they continued to work, their quality of life would increase because they had a different mindset and perspective. They did not have to stress about work or not being able to retire. They are now living the life they want because they can make choices that suit them. They know that they can advance to the next phase of their lives at any time because they have the financial resources to support them.

Up until that assessment, their biggest fear had been running out of money and what they would do when the paychecks stopped. Part of our role as financial planners is to explain to people the following: the paycheck does not stop. It just comes from a different source. Once enough money is amassed so that you are in a position to retire, a system can be set up whereby on a certain day every month, a certain amount is automatically deposited into your bank account just like a paycheck. The only difference is that this paycheck comes from assets, not from an employer. Understanding how that monthly deposit is generated and knowing they can depend on it made our clients feel secure, and it will do the same for you.

Once you are properly diversified, it's important not to let fear or greed drive decisions that affect that diversification. To do so indicates a failure to understand short-term, intermediate-term, and long-term money. If a stock, bond, or mutual fund is a long-term investment, and if the underlying investment is sound, then the right decision is to ride out the storm. If the investment is not sound, then it is time to move out of that investment and into something more appropriate for the long haul, not the short haul. Ultimately, being properly diversified is far more important than hanging on to or selling an investment out of fear or greed.

TAKEAWAY

→ When it comes to thinking about your financial future over a lifetime, you'll benefit by seeking outside advice from a seasoned financial advisor whose philosophy is broad diversification and disciplined, unemotional investing. Also, make sure that the financial advisor is looking at how the money is invested and who is managing the money first before looking at the rate of return.

→ When determining your financial picture, examine your debt load first; it dictates your next moves.

→ Money isn't just money. When you are investing, you should think of it as short-term, intermediate-term, and long-term money.

→ Doing so will help you make sure you have enough liquid money to cover expenses in the short and medium terms. This will allow you to both invest with confidence and avoid many common investment mistakes.

→ Rate of return is not as important as broad diversification.

→ You need to know who is managing the funds you invest in, how long they've been managing them, and if they have a significant amount of their own money invested in the mutual fund that they manage.

→ Break down your financial goals into incremental steps.

→ When you invest, you need to ride out market cycles, especially in times of financial crisis.

→ Investing should be a marathon, and diversification offers you the best path.

→ Don't make the mistake of being too diversified. Sitting down with a professional can help you figure out which investments are serving you best.

→ Fear and greed drive too many poor financial decisions. Once you learn how to think about money, they won't drive yours.

Now you're ready for a solid financial plan. In the next chapter, we'll discuss the other components that make up one.

CHAPTER 7

How to Build a Comprehensive Financial Plan

"**F**inancial planning" is a broad brush that covers many areas. Many people meet with advisors who tell them that financial planning is only investment planning or insurance planning or retirement planning. However, true comprehensive financial planning is like a pie with six pieces: investment planning, insurance planning and risk management, income tax planning, estate planning or wills and trusts, retirement planning, and college education planning (to the extent that there are children or grandchildren who need assistance).

Everyone should have a plan that looks at all six of these components. Here are some questions I'm going to answer in this chapter:

- What constitutes a comprehensive financial plan?

- How do you create this financial plan?

- Should you work with a financial planner?

- If you work with a financial planner, how much should you pay?

- How should all the pieces of the plan work together?

THE COMPREHENSIVE FINANCIAL PLAN

Many niche advisors specialize in one area but call themselves financial advisors. However, on closer inspection, it becomes clear that they are actually stockbrokers/investment advisors, insurance agents, estate planners, or income tax preparers. They might even be working for a bank as a private banker selling annuities. Today, saying, "I'm a financial planner," is like saying, "I'm a doctor," when what you really need to know is whether the person is a cardiologist or a dentist.

We have heard many potential clients say that they have been working with a financial planner but are not happy. That's usually because the advisor has not been doing comprehensive financial planning, where all the pieces of your plan are examined by someone who has the knowledge and capabilities to provide advice in all these areas.

For example, looking at only one piece of the plan would mean giving investment advice without understanding where the client stands in terms of income tax planning or risk tolerance. How can a decision be made with regard to retirement accounts or nonretirement accounts without knowing what the client's overall situation looks like? Furthermore, you can't determine the most efficient way to generate retirement income until you know how a client's holdings will be taxed. A knowledgeable financial advisor must know this in order to understand how much a client should take out of a nonretirement account versus a retirement account in order to minimize tax consequences while maximizing one's income stream.

In other words, the six different areas of the financial plan need to work in concert. If a planner has not done investment or retirement planning, then they have not planned for the client's long-term future. If they recommend putting away money into an investment account without looking at the client's overall life insurance need, the family's nest egg might be too small should the breadwinner die prematurely.

CREATING A FINANCIAL PLAN

Start by trying to consolidate all the components of your plan in the same place (or as few places as possible). Having an IRA with one or more firms; having your life insurance policies somewhere else; and owning a variety of stocks, bonds, and mutual funds that are held through various companies will make managing a financial plan quite challenging. It's important to get your arms wrapped around everything in an organized manner in order to figure out where you stand financially.

If you want to do your own financial planning, start by asking what you are trying to accomplish financially. Then put together a balance sheet to see where you are today. Start with your checking, savings, and money market accounts. Next check your investment accounts, such as mutual funds or annuities. Check to see whether you have any cash value life insurance. You can also see what's in your 401(k) or 403(b). On one side of the balance sheet, you should list all your assets, including home, cars, and collectibles. On the other side of the ledger, you should account for your debts: mortgage, credit card debt, car loans, and student loans.

This exercise helps you to build a picture of where you are today and allows you to decide what you do and do not like about this picture and why. You can look at each of the six financial plan components and see potential red flags.

Assessing your current financial state usually forces you to ask questions like these:

- Where do I want to be financially five years from now?

- How much do I need to have when I retire? And at what age would I like to be able to retire?

- If I die prematurely, how will my family be provided for?

- Is my will up to date?

- If I get sick and I'm incapacitated, who is authorized to make financial decisions on my part?

- Should I have a trust? If so, why?

Unfortunately, too many people come to our office and don't have answers to many of these questions. They often have no plan, do not know what their plan should be, or do not know when or if they can retire down the road. They do not know if they have too much life insurance or too little. They often think they are paying too much in income taxes and want to lower their tax bill.

This is why when we meet with new clients, we ask people to tell us where they are and what they like and dislike about where they are. This is a good starting place to design a financial plan.

Financial planning is complicated and can become overwhelming. People see so many pieces and parts that they begin to wonder how are they ever going to complete a plan. Perhaps that's where you are right now. You see where you are right now. You know where you want to be, but you cannot seem to figure out what steps need to be taken to get you on the right path. Or maybe you realize you're on the wrong path but don't know why or how to get onto the right one.

As a result, too many people see an ad on TV, or they talk to somebody who is selling life insurance, or they speak with a banker who's trying to sell them an annuity, and they get talked into buying a product instead of figuring out how all these pieces of a comprehensive financial plan work together.

A financial plan should be a finely tuned machine. The gears are different sizes and turn at different paces, but they all work together to help move that machine in the right direction. If one gear is not moving properly—for example, if your estate plan isn't up to date—and you die unexpectedly, your financial affairs might be tied up unnecessarily in probate court. Your family's life will have already been turned upside down because they lost a loved one. It shouldn't be made more complicated because you didn't have a current will, a current trust, or transfer-on-death provisions linked to how investments are owned.

The most important thing to consider when doing effective financial planning is that life is a marathon with twists and turns. Very often people focus on today and put off tomorrow. They work hard to earn money, but somewhere down the road, working life will stop, and they'll come to a place where they want to retire. Often, by the time they realize they have not planned for this day, it is too late; they have not planned to accumulate enough money and are not able to live as comfortably as they would like because they did not have a plan.

Plans have to be made and executed. They do not happen by themselves.

> Plans have to be made and executed. They do not happen by themselves.

WORKING WITH A FINANCIAL PLANNER

A good financial planner understands that each client's financial circumstances, goals, objectives, income levels, and tax bracket are different from other clients'. One of the advantages of working with a comprehensive financial planner is that they can help navigate you through the minefields. They can help plan ways to accomplish goals over time, so that somewhere down the road, you will have accumulated enough money so that you can retire and live comfortably, your children will have the college funds that they need, and your loved ones will have a trusted advisor who's not going to take advantage of them when you pass away and who will keep them on track.

A Blank Sheet of Paper

At our firm, we do not have any preconceived ideas when people walk in the door. We do not jump to conclusions about what investments they need or insurance they should carry, or what retirement or college education plan they should have. We come to the table with a blank sheet of paper to gather information so that we can help you figure out how to make all the various parts of the plan work together. We are like the conductor of an orchestra, navigating what notes each instrument should play so that all of the parts are working in unison. In this way, we can take the thirty-thousand-foot view to determine, among other factors, how clients can minimize their taxes, how much they should put into a 401(k), and how much they need to save in an after-tax investment account.

It is possible to work with a separate estate planning attorney, a CPA/tax preparer, a stockbroker/investment advisor, and a life insurance broker, but it is highly advisable that one person be the quarterback in order to properly coordinate all these elements. That way, if a client should die suddenly or become disabled, the plan will run smoothly. Or when a client is ready to retire, he or she has the means to do so.

We have seen clients who worked with an estate planning attorney and had great wills and trust documents. On the other hand, their estate planning attorney had not worked with the insurance broker, the investment advisor, or the financial advisor to make sure that the assets were properly titled and the beneficiaries were properly designated.

Ideally, you should have either a financial planner who handles all the elements of a financial plan or one who coordinates the effort with specialists in each area. That person can look at all the moving parts as a whole. The key is to have knowledgeable people in each area and one financial planner who makes sure they are communicating with each other, whether the team members are under the umbrella of one firm or individuals in outside firms. This is a complex task that requires choosing a properly qualified financial planner, not just an investment or insurance advisor.

> Ideally, you should have either a financial planner who handles all the elements of a financial plan or one who coordinates the effort with specialists in each area.

RECOGNIZING A QUALIFIED FINANCIAL PLANNER

One way to distinguish between a financial planner and a financial advisor is to check for certification. The College for Financial Planning has a certification program for Certified Financial Planners. A Certified Financial Planner (CFP®) must adhere to a fiduciary standard; the planner must take a series of courses, must meet certain accreditation and continuing education requirements, and must abide by a code of ethics that states they must always put clients' interests first.

Do your due diligence to ensure that the planner you select is indeed competent and ethical. This is true in all professions: financial planning, legal, medical. There are good and bad planners. They do not have to be a CFP® to be a good planner, and being certified does not guarantee that they are a good comprehensive planner. Nevertheless, a CFP® designation does indicate that this individual has the CFP® educational background and is supposed to meet and abide by certain accreditation requirements.

Ask a potential CFP® about their approach and area or areas of expertise. This will help you understand what to expect, whether their approach to planning will be tailored to you, or whether it will have a scope limited to certain products—for example, life insurance or annuity products. It is also advisable to ask how they charge for their advice. After all, these fees are coming out of your investment returns directly or indirectly.

THE COST OF ADVICE

Charlie, a longtime client of mine, called one day to say that I might be hearing from John, his golfing buddy. While they were playing golf, they got around to talking about their investments, the market, and their rates of return. Every time they had this conversation on the golf course, John realized his investments were not doing as well as Charlie's. Neither could quite pinpoint why, so one day, Charlie suggested that John should call me to get a second opinion.

When John called, he admitted that he did not believe he was getting the same kind of advice as Charlie, and unlike Charlie, his investments were lagging, but he didn't know why. We told him that we would be happy to take a look at his investments, asked him to bring in a variety of documents and statements to review, and invited him in for an initial meeting a week later.

When John came in, we spent some time getting to know a little about him and finding out a bit more about his concerns. Then we asked the following question: "How much are you paying for the advice you are getting?" He replied that he was paying less than most people because he was getting the "friends and family discount," which he clarified to mean that a good friend at a major brokerage firm had been helping him for the last fifteen years. He showed me on his statements that he was paying an advisory fee of 1.25 percent of his assets each year. After glancing at his statement, we also noticed that he had a series of mutual funds that were not necessarily funds we would use or recommend to clients.

He gave us permission to have one of our staff members run a detailed analysis report from Morningstar, an independent research service that evaluates mutual funds. Morningstar has a report called "Portfolio Snapshot" that shows the investment mix of the portfolio, its historic performance compared to the benchmarks, and the internal mutual fund expenses embedded in the mutual fund portfolio. All mutual funds have internal management fees, costs, and charges.

It turned out that the internal mutual fund expenses for his portfolio were 1.1 percent annually. This meant that in addition to the 1.25 percent in advisory fees that were reflected on his investment statements, he was also paying another 1.1 percent in internal management fees to the mutual funds inside his portfolio. His total cost was actually 2.35 percent a year, an amount of which he was unaware.

In recent years, there has been a lot of controversy over how advisors get compensated for the advice they provide. We told John, as we do all our potential clients, that their total cost, direct and indirect, should be approximately 1 percent per year or lower. Our definition of **total cost** includes the internal cost inside the underlying mutual fund investments on an annual basis as well as what the advisor charges in advisory fees. By industry standards, our fees are extremely low.

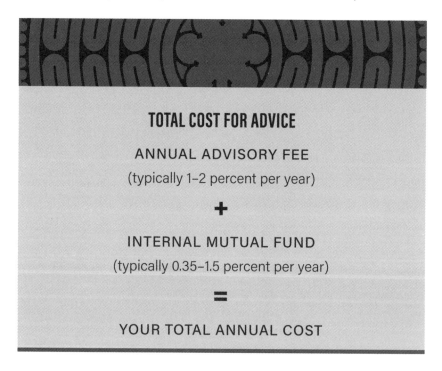

TOTAL COST FOR ADVICE

ANNUAL ADVISORY FEE
(typically 1–2 percent per year)

+

INTERNAL MUTUAL FUND
(typically 0.35–1.5 percent per year)

=

YOUR TOTAL ANNUAL COST

Until then, John, like many investors, had seen only the number visible on his statements and had blindly assumed that was what advice was costing him. No one is actually lying here. The mutual fund companies do disclose these internal expenses. They are just hard to find in the prospectus. The result, however, was that John was never going to get the same rate of return as my client Charlie because he was being charged more than double the cost for advice. Seeing the total cost of fees and advice was an eye-opening experience that resulted in John becoming a client of Chornyak & Associates.

We have met many clients like John who come to us because

they are dissatisfied with the advice they are receiving and the fees they've been paying for the advice. We ask them how much they've been paying their advisor, and they usually say 1 percent or 1.25 percent, sometimes even 2 percent. However, when we drill down into their portfolios and see their total costs, we always find that this is only what they are paying the advisor of the firm with which they are affiliated. There is an additional layer of fees they do not see, such as the 0.5–1.2 percent internal expenses on their mutual funds. This means the client ends up spending a total of 2 percent or 3 percent a year in fees, which can dramatically affect the performance of their portfolio and overall financial plan. When we look at this, we tell them that they are paying too much, and we advise them to take a holistic view of their overall financial plan to get these fees down to approximately 1 percent or lower.

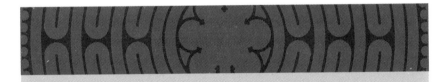

FEES MATTER

Pay attention to your *total* annual cost.

Investor A invests $100,000 and earns a 6 percent return each year for twenty years but pays 2 percent in annual fees. They will end up with $222,258 after paying $108,762 in costs.

Investor B invests $100,000 and earns a 6 percent return each year for twenty years, but only pays 1 percent in annual fees. They will end up with $271,264 after paying $59,756 in costs.

Which investor do you want to be?

TAKEAWAY

A financial plan is made up of six parts, and while each part moves separately, it needs to be coordinated as a whole.

These days, many advisors say they are managing a client's portfolio or selling insurance based on the client's needs, without looking at the overarching picture of whether these parts all work together or against each other or whether the client's family is left wide open for losses or probate expenses should the client die prematurely.

The most comprehensive and efficient approach is to work with one financial planner who can either oversee all the components of a plan as they are being managed within his or her company or can make sure everyone is talking to each other if the client is working with separate advisors, attorneys, and brokers.

This person can also make sure that the fees paid are not eroding the return on the client's investments. Ultimately, all the pieces of the financial plan need to be linked in the planning process.

Make sure you know how much you're paying for the advice you are getting. The percentage you see may tell only part of the story. Find out what fees may be hidden or buried in the fine print.

As you can probably tell by now, I'm passionate about financial planning and believe that it's important to have absolute transparency on the part of the planner. I hope this chapter has both informed you and excited you to want to know more about each part of the plan. That's what we're going to do next.

CHAPTER 8

How to Think about Life Insurance

L ife insurance, in its broadest sense, is designed and intended to replace a loss of income, usually in the event that the breadwinner dies prematurely.

Think of the breadwinner as a money machine. Every day they get up, go to work, and generate income. The money that they earn goes into their bank account to cover all their living expenses and whatever future expenses they expect.

When they are alive, they are generating an income, supporting their family, and giving to their churches and/or favorite causes. They may be helping parents, saving for children's college, and hopefully amassing enough money to provide an income after retirement so they do not have to be money machines long after they want to stop working. However, if they die before they've amassed enough to meet their goals and objectives for the long term, the life insurance proceeds can step in and cover the loss of income in a cash payout.

There are many different types of life insurance and many

different opinions as to the appropriate amount of life insurance that one should actually have. Now we're going to look at the different types of life insurance available, how to determine how much insurance is enough, and, just as important, how *not* to think about life insurance.

As you know, life insurance provides an injection of money to take care of loved ones when the breadwinner is no longer here to do so. It replaces the money that you would otherwise accumulate over time if you were alive. This means the need for life insurance for most people is finite. Thus, your need for life insurance is greater in your younger years and smaller as retirement age approaches (assuming that you've been saving along the way). Think of life insurance as a conduit between today, when you don't have enough money to retire, and the day when you do.

> Your need for life insurance is greater in your younger years and smaller as retirement age approaches.

A second way to think about life insurance is as a legacy for children and grandchildren, or charities if you have philanthropic goals you want to see fulfilled in the event you are not alive to do that yourself. If, for example, someone has been living on a retirement fund for a long time before passing, there might not be much left at the time of death. In this case, a block of life insurance can provide a cash payout to children, grandchildren, or a nonprofit organization. As such, life insurance is actually death insurance. It is intended to fill a financial void if somebody dies before they can take care of their family or leave a financial legacy.

Although life insurance is necessary, you need to ask yourself what you want it to accomplish for you. What assets do you already have, and how much would you need to take care of your family if you died and your income ceased? Further, how long would your family need this additional money? If you have other assets, there will likely be an income stream that will continue to flow to your spouse or children should you die prematurely. This means, for most people, life insurance is temporary. Unfortunately, all too often, people get talked into buying high-premium cash value building life insurance products that are designed to pay the insurance agent a big commission but are not necessarily in the best interest of the consumer. This is where understanding the types of life insurance available becomes important.

TYPES OF LIFE INSURANCE

In its broadest sense, there are two kinds of life insurance. The first is death-benefit-only life insurance or term life insurance, which pays something out when you die. The second is cash value building life insurance.

Term Life Insurance

Term life insurance is the cheapest form of life insurance in terms of annual premium and is the least expensive way of providing protection for your family for the length of time they need it.

In taking out a term life policy, the buyer enters into a contract with the insurance company to pay, for example, $1,000 a year in premium for a twenty-year policy in exchange for $500,000 worth of death benefit. The premium is larger when the policyholder is older or in poor health because the odds that the insurance company will have to pay out the death benefit are higher.

Term insurance provides a death benefit only. It does not build up cash value. Essentially, in exchange for a guaranteed level premium for twenty years, the insurance company provides, for example, a $500,000 level death benefit in the event of death within those twenty years. In this case, you know the premium, the death benefit, and how long the insurance company is on the hook to pay the death benefit. At the end of twenty years, the coverage will stop (sometimes the premiums can continue at a much higher premium). However, with proper planning, enough should have been accumulated in retirement accounts and investments by then so that the term policy is no longer needed. Effectively, you have reached a point where you are self-insured. The length of this type of policy is typically between ten and thirty years.

Cash Value Life Insurance

Cash value building life insurance products include whole life, variable life, and variable universal life, among other types. These policies are like forced savings. You pay a higher premium per year in exchange for internal cash accumulation and a death benefit that will in many cases last longer than a term insurance policy, as long as the premiums are paid or there is sufficient cash value in the policy.

For example, a whole life policy refers to a policy on which premiums are paid until the end of the insured's life and where the death benefit is guaranteed for life. Unlike term insurance, a twenty-year, limited-pay life policy means paying higher premiums for twenty years (and then stopping future premiums), but the death benefit is there for the insured's life.

This type of life insurance product appeals to people who believe that they need life insurance regardless of how long they live. It allows them to pass something on to their heirs, in the form of a death benefit, no matter at what age they die. For example, one of our clients wanted to make sure that each of his grandchildren received $1 million when he died, irrespective of what other assets he had. He bought a $3 million life insurance policy and pays a premium every year, which he will do for the rest of his life in order to guarantee the grandchildren will each get $1 million upon his death. This policy, therefore, builds up cash inside the policy through higher premiums. If he lives to be one hundred, for all practical purposes, he will have paid enough in that he will have self-funded that $3 million policy, but if he dies prematurely, the insurance company will make up the difference.

For most individuals, regular term insurance properly set up is the most appropriate because it is the least expensive way to protect against a premature death of the breadwinner. However, as with our client above, there are reasons to have a cash accumulation policy, depending on your goals and objectives. Nevertheless, in today's world, there are often better investment alternatives available to grow your assets for retirement, which we will look at shortly.

THE CHANGING MARKETPLACE

Over the last forty years, the life insurance industry has transformed, largely due to technology and insurance companies pricing their products more competitively.

Back in the 1950s, 1960s, and 1970s, life insurance was sold as a way for people to protect their family and accumulate a cash savings inside the policy that could be used instead of the death benefit. Therefore, it had living benefits in that part of the premiums that went into the policy could be invested by the insurance company inside the policy to grow on a tax-deferred basis. People bought a life insurance policy with the understanding that it accumulated cash value, which they could tap into at some later date when they needed it.

Since then, the financial industry evolved with the growth of mutual funds, the expansion of retirement benefits, 401(k)s and 403(b)s, and the advent of IRAs that allowed people to put money away for retirement. As a result, the insurance industry had to evolve because more and more people were asking whether the cash value build-up was really a good investment compared to these other new alternatives.

Over the years, there has been a shift away from cash accumulation life insurance—once called permanent insurance—to buying just death-benefit-only or term life insurance.

The death-benefit-only concept has become more prevalent because consumers who have a need for the insurance realize that, after a certain amount of time, they will have accumulated enough assets to take care of themselves and their families without needing to have a life insurance policy to offset a financial loss. The trend now is to provide a level premium and a level death benefit for a period of years—for example, ten, fifteen, twenty, or thirty years. Premiums are lower because there is no cash value involved, and no savings are being accumulated inside a term insurance policy.

Cash value products are still offered, oftentimes with lots of bells and whistles, but it is extremely rare that a cash value policy is a better long-term investment than a properly diversified investment portfolio coupled with a term policy for the appropriate length of time that it's needed. We'll look at an example of this in the next section. In short, cash value life insurance tends to be a low yielding investment, which is why we typically advise clients to use life insurance for its intended purpose—to provide a death benefit.

HOW MUCH IS ENOUGH?

When deciding on life insurance, the first question is, "How much do I need based on what I'm trying to accomplish?" The second question is, "How long do I need it?" For example, young people may not have much wealth accumulated, which means the life insurance death benefit needs to be big enough to take care of dependents. However, as they get older and have more money in a retirement account and other investment accounts, their nest egg will eventually be big enough so that they do not need life insurance to protect their loved ones. Then they can live on what they've accumulated, and when they pass on, their heirs can live on that money too.

How Much Is Needed?

Determining how much is needed requires taking a close look at the balance sheet. As I pointed out in the last chapter on financial planning, investors need to assess their assets and liabilities and overall financial picture. They need to look at the assets and the resources that would be available to generate an income for their family if they were no longer here, including money market accounts, retirement accounts, social security survivor benefits, their personal and group life insurance, etc.

Next, they must deduct costs that are incurred upon their death—for example, medical bills that are not covered by insurance. It is advisable to allocate $10,000 to this expense (assuming that you have health insurance). Funeral expenses also need to be factored in, which could be another $10,000–$20,000. Legal costs involved in settling the estate could amount to another $5,000–$10,000.

Take the assets and the resources that you have and total them up. Then reduce that figure by the expenses associated with your death above, and you'll have the net amount that will be left to the family. This is what they have to live on for the rest of their lives.

Next, figure out what these net assets will earn each year. This is the income that the family should have available to live on without depleting the assets. A properly diversified investment portfolio should be able to earn 5 percent per year long term. By way of example, if there are $1 million in assets earning 5 percent, the family will have an additional $50,000 a year in income from the investment assets to live on. If children are minors, there may also be additional monthly benefits available to the family from social security or from a social security or other governmental survivor benefit for a spouse who becomes eligible as early as age sixty. These should be factored in as well.

This assessment shows you what the family has to live on if the breadwinner passes away and that income was lost tomorrow. From this, it is possible to identify if there will be a shortfall between the income and expenses that the family needs to cover. By going through this exercise, the breadwinner is able to assess if he or she has enough life insurance or if more needs to be added.

How Long Is It Needed?

Financial projections can help you decide how long you need to carry life insurance. If you determine that you will accumulate enough money to retire in fifteen years, then we would recommend that you have enough life insurance to cover you for twenty years. Even though you might only need to keep the life insurance for fifteen years, unexpected things happen. Therefore, we like to add the extra five years as a buffer. That buffer will help you sleep at night if there is a downturn in the market or your nest egg grows slower than projected.

Everyone has different goals and objectives, and these need to be identified before assessing how much insurance needs to be carried to meet them and for how long.

At the end of the hypothetical fifteen-year period, if you have managed your financial affairs properly, you will have accumulated enough to cover the payout of the insurance policy. By that time, you get to a point where you no longer need to work or are only working because you want to. As a result, your life insurance needs will have dropped off dramatically. Again, you will no longer need to carry it because your assets will generate enough income without the insurance.

HOW NOT TO THINK ABOUT LIFE INSURANCE

Life insurance has advantages in a business setting for much the same reason as it does in one's family. It's needed when the premature death of an executive could have an adverse effect on business, especially a small business. Similarly, a business may also need life insurance for key employees to ensure there is sufficient cash flow during a business transition if one of them dies.

Great Policy—but Not for the Client

A potential client came to us a few years ago and said he was working with a financial planner. He had a "special" type of retirement plan and was spending over $14,000 a year on a life insurance policy that was also going to provide him with retirement income. Does that sound too good to be true? Well, on inspection, it turned out he had a very expensive policy with large surrender charges. It was far more expensive than just going out and buying a regular term insurance policy that would have cost less than $1,000 and would have allowed him to take the difference of over $13,000 a year and invest it in higher yielding long-term investments. That's right. We're talking about the difference between $1,000 and $14,000 a year.

The supposed financial advisor convinced him to use cash value life insurance as a retirement accumulation investment vehicle. The only real benefit to the cash value policy was that he would get the death benefit, but he had paid too much for this. When it comes to cash value insurance, after factoring in internal fees, expenses, surrender charges, and the embedded costs, there are many better investment products in the marketplace. The financial advisor was in reality a life insurance salesman selling a very high commission policy that was in his best interest rather than in the client's best interest. We'll look at these later in the book.

In the current regulatory climate, insurance agents are treated differently than securities licensed individuals. A broker can be licensed to sell securities, mutual funds, and many different types of investments, but not necessarily life insurance. That client who came to us under the impression that he was using a life insurance product as a long-term retirement investment had only succeeded in carrying a policy that was great for the insurance company and the agent who sold it to him for a handsome commission, but it was not a great investment for him. The commissions that the agent made only helped the agent—not the client!

TAKEAWAY

→ The best way to think about life insurance is as a death benefit vehicle that will take care of the family or a philanthropic endeavor after you pass on. Once you identify the insurance goals, you should look for the least expensive premium that meets them.

→ Unfortunately, people can get talked into buying something far more expensive with far more strings attached. This is good for the insurance company and the insurance agent because they make fees and commissions, but it is rarely good for the consumer. When it comes to buying insurance, come back to the basics and ask, "How much do I need, and how long do I need it?"

→ When it comes to life insurance, the best advice is to periodically look at how close you are to reaching your goals and objectives. Today, you may need $500,000 or $1 million of life insurance, but ten years from now, you may have $300,000 in assets, leaving you with the reduced need for only $200,000 to $700,000 of life insurance. In fifteen years, this will be less, and in twenty years, you may need no life insurance at all because you may have accumulated enough assets to self-insure to meet your goals and objectives.

→ Think of life insurance not as an investment vehicle but as insurance in the event of premature death, which is its intended purpose.

We've been talking about retirement a lot in this chapter and in this book. Now we're going to take a closer look.

CHAPTER 9

How to Think about Your Retirement

R etirement means different things to different people. For those who worked all their lives, it is the light at the end of the proverbial tunnel that brings the day when they are able to stop working and do what they really want to do for the rest of their lives. Perhaps for you, it's to travel, to give back to the community, or to start a second career. Some clients want to retire yesterday because they do not like what they do or because they want to redirect their time and energy toward other interests. Other clients never want to stop working.

NOT AN AGE

Retirement is not an age but a goal. It is the point in time when people have accumulated enough money after a period of years of investing it properly and conservatively so that they can draw a line in the sand and say, "I have accumulated enough now so that if I wanted to stop working, if I wanted to change my career path, if I wanted to stop being an attorney or an engineer or a schoolteacher, and take up painting or working at the library or donating time to the local hospital or church or just traveling to see the world, I can." Retirement is a personal choice. There is no hard and fast rule that anyone must retire at a given age.

> Retirement is a personal choice. There is no hard and fast rule that anyone must retire at a given age.

When you think about retirement, you need to think about what would make you happy and what you would want to do if you were not working. The next question then is how can you get there from where you currently are? In order to meet your goals, you need to know how to think about your retirement funds. In this chapter, I want to focus on the broad areas that affect most people saving for retirement: how to think about taxation as it relates to retirement savings, employer matching contributions, and when to start taking your social security benefits.

PAY NOW OR PAY LATER

Many people who do not work with a financial planner do an excellent job of putting a lot of pretax money into their retirement accounts. Taxes are not paid on any of the earnings of those investments at first because they grow on a tax-deferred basis. In these accounts, it is typically not possible to access money without penalties before age 59½. The downside of these accounts is that while taxes are not paid every year on the compounding growth, when the money is pulled out upon retirement, it is all taxed as ordinary income rather than the lower long-term capital gains tax rates that would have been paid had taxes been paid outside the account in the years the money was being contributed.

In other words, there is no free lunch. The government does not give away anything. While you may not be paying taxes as you're earning returns on your retirement savings investments, you'll have to pay those taxes down the road. Depending on your tax bracket, you could actually end up in a higher tax bracket if your retirement accounts have significantly grown as pretax savings rather than your savings in a taxable account on which you paid taxes each year. And if you don't spend all the money in your retirement accounts while you're alive, your heirs may very well pay higher taxes when they inherit what's left in your retirement accounts.

In nonretirement accounts, which are individual investment accounts, taxes are paid on dividends and realized capital gains every year, but at a lower tax rate than that applicable to ordinary income. Currently, the income tax structure gives significantly more favorable tax treatment to qualified dividends and long-term capital gains.

In my opinion, it is important to accumulate two separate buckets of investments: in one, money that has already been taxed is invested, and taxes are paid yearly on the dividends and realized capital gains earned each year but at a lower tax rate; in the other, contributions are invested on a pretax basis, and the taxes are deferred until retirement.

Having two buckets helps people think and plan long term in a tax-efficient manner. If a person puts all their money into a pretax retirement account and none into an after-tax investment account, they'll oftentimes end up paying more taxes when they reach retirement. Every time money is taken from an account that has not had taxes paid on it—for example, to help grandchildren with college or buy a new car or take a vacation—the retiree has to withdraw more than is actually needed because the government will take a slice of it for taxes. For example, if you need $20,000, you will need to withdraw approximately $30,000 pretax because you will owe approximately 30 percent in taxes. Withdrawing this higher amount also pushes people into a higher tax bracket. This is a tax trap into which many people fall.

Many people remember the Fram Oil Filter commercial slogan: "Pay me now or pay me later." The commercial said that if someone avoided changing their oil filter today and did not change their oil periodically, eventually their engine would blow up. If they did not pay small amounts regularly to take care of their car now, they ultimately ended up paying a lot more later. This is the same with retirement accounts. You can pay now or pay later. Saving in both types of accounts makes a more flexible retirement investment plan.

EMPLOYER MATCHING FUNDS

Many people work for companies where the employer matches up to 6 percent of whatever the employee puts into their 401(k) account. Some companies match dollar for dollar, and others match fifty or seventy-five cents for every dollar employees contribute. This is bonus money that every employee should try to take full advantage of until they've maxed out the employer match. For example, if your employer provides a match on the first 6 percent of your earnings that you contribute, then you should try to contribute 6 percent in order to get the match. Think of it as free money.

SOCIAL SECURITY

Social security has three different timelines: early retirement, which can start as early as age sixty-two; full retirement, which falls somewhere between ages sixty-six and sixty-seven, depending on the employee's date of birth; and mandatory retirement distributions, which are paid starting at age seventy-two.

The driver behind the decision to take social security early or later depends on whether you are going to continue to work. The monthly benefit at age sixty-two is smaller than the monthly benefit at age sixty-six, and the monthly benefit at age sixty-six is smaller than the monthly benefit at age seventy-two. It is a matter of mathematics. The monthly benefit is bigger later because the government will be paying out the monthly benefit for a shorter period of time because your remaining years on this earth are fewer.

Between early retirement and full retirement, you can start drawing a reduced social security benefit. If you have earnings from employment of less than approximately $18,000 in a calendar year, then drawing early social security retirement may make sense. If you will continue to earn more than $18,000 a year from employment, it might make sense to not take it early because you will have to pay some of your social security benefit back based on how much you earn.

Therefore, the question becomes, After age sixty-two, will you be employed? If so, how much will you be earning? What a person will be earning drives when they should begin withdrawing social security. If they wait until their full retirement age, they can start drawing the monthly benefit without having an offset reduction from employment income if they continue to work. For example, a sixty-eight-year-old can earn $300,000 a year in employment income and still collect their full social security on top of that without having to give back any of it.

You can see how the pieces of financial planning are starting to come together and how you can't really assemble a plan until you understand all of these pieces.

TAKEAWAY

→ Don't retire just because you have enough money to retire. Instead, retire because you have something else in your life you want to do.

→ Try to accumulate in both tax-deferred and after-tax accounts.

→ A good retirement plan should provide everyone with the flexibility they need to make decisions that are best for them as life goes on.

→ When it comes to thinking about retiring, it is best to put money away as early as possible to give it time to grow.

→ Every employee should assess their balance sheet to see how much they have in assets and how much income those assets will continue to generate over time. These numbers help them focus on their priorities.

No matter how much you earn, you must still think about and plan for taxes, and that's what we're going to look at next.

CHAPTER 10

How to Do Tax Planning

A new client came to us recently with a pile of papers, income statements, expenses, distributions, and retirement accounts and asked what we could do to reduce their tax bill. However, because this data was being presented after their income and expenses had been earned and spent and investment decisions had been made, the scope for reducing their tax burden was limited. They had not been working with a financial planner and had a cursory relationship with their tax preparer, with whom they met only once a year to prepare their tax returns for the previous tax year.

Very often clients come to a financial planner or a CPA only during tax season, hoping to defer or eliminate a portion of their prior year's tax liability. There are some things that can be done to lower their tax liability. That said, detailed tax planning in advance is always preferable.

At Chornyak & Associates, we ask new clients to provide us

with their last two years' income tax returns—federal, state, and local—and all their supporting documents as part of our data-gathering process. We review and audit these returns in conjunction with tax professionals to make sure that the prior year's returns have been accurately prepared. This also helps us establish their current year's income tax bracket and tax liability and what impact this may have on future investment decisions. At our firm, this is critical to effective comprehensive financial planning, which includes tax planning.

TWO TYPES OF TAX PREPARERS

First, you need to understand that there are two types of tax preparers. The first takes the clients' historic data and simply puts the information on the tax forms. They do not do a lot in terms of trying to reduce the actual tax liability. The second type of tax preparer takes a forward-planning approach and offers ongoing communication and dialogue during the current tax year. This eliminates surprises on April 15 because the client's best outcome is planned well in advance according to set goals for a given calendar year.

Often, we refer clients to an outside CPA. You might think of it as having your family physician managing your care and sending you to specialists as needed. Although our firm has an extensive tax background, including CPAs on staff, we like to be the last ones to go over every detail. I can say in all honesty that we typically know more about our clients than anyone else. More than their accountant, attorney, doctor, and perhaps even their spouse. We become the second set of eyes that reviews the tax return for our clients.

Whalen & Company, a highly reputable firm with more than seventy years of experience, works with many of our clients. In this chapter, I'd like to lift the veil and show you—with the help of Lisa Shuneson, CPA, and Richard Crabtree, CPA, comanaging partners at Whalen & Company, whom I interviewed for this chapter—what happens in such a consultation. It's as close as I can bring you to the actual experience, and I hope you find it helpful.

During our first meeting with the client I mentioned above, we looked through their paperwork to understand their lifestyle, their situation, the decisions they made, and the team with which they had worked. As with all our clients, our goal is to communicate with them and understand their long-term goals and dreams as we establish and build an ongoing relationship. As part of our process, we often engage the services of Lisa and Richard at Whalen & Company. As I mentioned earlier, if you work with a financial planner who partners with seasoned tax professionals to do forward planning, you'll increase the odds of achieving your investment objectives, and you'll be supported by a wise tax strategy.

As with almost all people who think about taxation after the fact, the client's first meeting at Whalen & Company offered a somewhat limited scope for ways to reduce their prior year's tax liability. Their situation was one Richard and Lisa call "closed transactions"—that is, all the activity and the financial transactions had already been completed for the prior tax year. So the tax planning strategies for the prior year were limited.

However, in terms of planning for the current tax year, they were able to establish a relationship and work in conjunction with us to plan ahead and advise the client on the tax implications of decisions they were contemplating, transactions they were considering, and their plans for retirement. As a team, we were then able to do real long-range planning and suggest adjustments according to changes in their goals and circumstances as they arose throughout the year and beyond. We will look at these strategies in more detail in this chapter. First, though, let's talk about tax planning.

WHAT IS TAX PLANNING?

Tax planning is the process of arranging financial affairs to minimize tax liabilities. There is nothing inherently illegal or immoral in the avoidance of taxation as long as it is within the tax system's rules.

Tax planning can be divided into two major categories: open transactions and closed transactions.

Open Transactions

In an open transaction, the tax specialist can maintain some degree of control of a client's tax liability because their transactions have not been completed—for example, an anticipated stock liquidation or property that has not been sold yet. This allows the tax specialist to review the different circumstances around a transaction and make favorable tax recommendations. We will discuss some examples of these situations later in this chapter.

Closed Transactions

A closed transaction situation, however, is one where all the transactions are completed, which is the case at the end of the tax year when tax returns need to be prepared. This limits what a tax preparer can do to reduce the client's tax bill.

There are always more opportunities to offer people tax reduction alternatives in their everyday affairs and decisions in advance. This means that the first requirement for effective tax planning comes from tax awareness on the part of clients by communicating with their financial planner and/or their tax professional as early as possible. We will look at this in more detail at the end of this chapter. An effective client–tax planner relationship based on education and forward planning will encourage the client to identify financial goals and the general means to achieve them and afford him or her more control over making good decisions in areas that have tax consequences. This, in turn, offers the financial planner and the tax professional more creativity in devising tax-efficient strategies.

In short, effective tax planning requires that the client, the financial planner, and the tax specialist have ongoing dialogue and be proactively involved in the tax implications of financial and lifestyle change decisions throughout the year. This dialogue should also include other members of the client's financial planning team.

THE BENEFITS OF FORWARD PLANNING

Knowing the client is an important and often overlooked aspect of the client–tax specialist relationship. Understanding a client's lifestyle and goals can be very helpful in identifying tax savings in their everyday decisions in advance. Even knowing where a client lives and works can yield tax savings.

For example, one of our clients lives in a nontax municipality and worked in a tax municipality in Ohio. His employer withheld 2.5 percent last year from his earnings in municipality taxes. However, the client worked remotely from home six months of the year, which meant he was eligible for a refund of half this municipal tax. He earned $200,000 a year and therefore paid $5,000 in municipal taxes, $2,500 of which was refunded. These savings are often overlooked when tax preparers focus only on the federal tax return.

> Knowing the client is an important and often overlooked aspect of the client–tax specialist relationship.

Changes in a client's circumstances need to be factored into every forward plan, and it is important that the client and tax specialist have an open dialogue so that these issues are communicated to produce tax-efficient planning. Some of these circumstances that have tax implications would be an increase in income because of a bonus, the exercising of a stock option, a change of jobs, or a spouse beginning employment.

When a client loses their job and gets a severance package, their tax picture often changes that year. Therefore, they need to make their tax professional aware of the details of the severance package because significant tax planning can be done to benefit the individual during a time of job transition.

For example, one client was terminated and given a six-month severance package. The year he was terminated, he would be working only nine of the twelve months and would not be entitled to his end-of-year bonus. This made his income significantly lower that tax year. In addition, because he was no longer contributing to his employer's 401(k), his taxable income went up. Lisa and Richard advised him to go back to his employer and adjust his withholding so that it would more accurately reflect what he should have been withholding that year overall. In this way, instead of having too much withheld and then being entitled to a big tax refund the following April, his take-home pay was increased in the present, giving him more disposable income during his job transition period.

You must also consider tax implications when exercising stocks. Executives are often given stock options as part of their long-term compensation. These stock options have a time limit on when they can be exercised. For example, an employee might have received stock options when his employer's company stock was worth forty dollars a share, with a five-year vesting schedule to buy the shares. If the shares appreciate to sixty dollars two years later, the executive stands to make a profit should he or she exercise their right to purchase the vested shares. This, however, is something he or she should discuss with his or her tax planner and financial planner in advance of exercising the stock options to understand the potential tax liability the following April. There may be ways to offset or reduce the tax liability.

Another client of ours owned an investment that he had held for fewer than twelve months and that had appreciated significantly during that time. He wanted to sell the investment to lock in the gain. However, much of this gain would have been taxed at the much higher short-term tax rate on this short-term gain, since he had not held the investment for more than twelve months. In conjunction with Richard and Lisa, we worked with this client in advance to ensure that he understood that if he held the investment for more than twelve months, the tax liability would be significantly lower because the gain would be taxed at the lower long-term capital-gain tax rate.

Another couple came to us during tax season the year after the wife returned to work. She had been out of the workforce for some time. As a dual-income family, the withholding on the husband's paycheck didn't factor in the tax implications of his wife's additional income. When filing jointly at the end of the year, they were in a higher tax bracket than they had been when he was the sole wage earner. Since they hadn't planned properly, they had underwithheld and found themselves with a large tax balance due when they filed their tax return.

It is important to remember that if you have a change in your income, either up or down, to plan accordingly in advance so that you don't have surprises on April 15. We gather the information so that when there is a change (a client goes back to work, or on the opposite end of the spectrum, a client loses a job, has unemployment or severance, or retires), we can figure out what needs to be adjusted in order to minimize their tax liability. We don't like our clients having surprises, not even big tax refunds. "I got a big refund" only means that "I gave the government an interest-free loan."

Part of the responsibility of the tax specialist is to plan for these situations. A good tax planner will monitor a client's data during the year and as necessary update his or her income tax projection for that current calendar year. With each update, the tax specialist should offer advice on when to increase or decrease withholding, for example, or prepay items, defer a bonus, or increase charitable contributions to offset the tax liability of a spike in income. However, without communicating clearly with your tax planner to do forward planning, you could end up with surprises at tax time. Therefore, having an ongoing dialogue with tax planners and making sure they are part of the larger financial planning team is crucial to your financial plan.

3 KEYS TO TAX PLANNING

Tax planning is a complex process that needs to be tailored to each client's needs. However, when it comes to having a solid tax plan as part of an overall financial plan, the first three areas to be reviewed from a tax planning perspective are timing, deductions, and credits.

Timing

There are certain instances where the timing of a decision can reap substantial tax benefits. Sometimes the client has control over these decisions, such as when receiving a bonus at work. A bonus is recognized as income in the tax year it is received. If, for example, a client expects to have lower income the following year, he or she should take the bonus the following year or split it across years if that is possible. Thus, good timing in terms of receiving the bonus can have tax benefits.

Timing is also important in portfolio management. If, in the middle of a tax year, a client invested in a stock or mutual fund that appreciated in value two months later, he or she may have a decision to make with regard to its sale. The timing of the sale dictates how the gain will be treated for tax purposes. If the stock is sold in fewer than twelve months of buying it, significantly higher income taxes will be owed on the profit. However, selling the stock after twelve months will result in paying less in taxes because of the lower long-term capital gains tax rate. There can be a significant variance between those two rates. If the sale is timed correctly, the investor's tax bill on the gain could be cut in half or even to zero depending on the investor's overall income level that year.

Other clients have benefited by correctly timing the sale of their homes or another property that may not qualify for exclusion as a personal residence. Timing the sale correctly could result in the long-term capital gains rates being applied versus the higher ordinary tax rates. This is a permanent tax savings if handled properly.

Deductions

When lawmakers change the tax code, tax planners must adjust their approach to tax planning.

Prior to 2018, most people either itemized their deductions every year or bundled expenses and itemized deductions one year and took the standard deduction the next to take advantage of prevailing tax thresholds. However, in 2018, the standard deduction for federal taxes was almost doubled to $12,000 for individuals and $24,000 for married couples, making it more beneficial for many taxpayers to take the standard deduction instead of itemizing. Add to this the bundling of state income taxes, local income taxes, and real estate taxes into one category with a cap of $10,000. In other words, while the standard deduction for a couple was $24,000, if a client chose to itemize their deductions, only $10,000 of the total state, local, and real estate taxes they paid could be deducted on the federal tax return.

In light of the new higher standard deductions and the $10,000 cap on deductibility of state, local, and real estate taxes, careful planning can help those who are philanthropic because you might be able to bundle your donations in one year or set up a charitable foundation that gives you the ability to put multiple years of donations into a single tax year.

Coming up with deductions that exceed the combined $24,000 standard deduction (for a married couple) in order to benefit from itemizing deductions can be challenging for clients. For example, one of our clients owns a valuable home and is in a high-income bracket. He pays more than $300,000 a year in state, local, and real estate taxes. Prior to 2018, he had a very large itemized deduction on his income tax return, but since 2018, he is limited to a $10,000 deduction. He and his wife had no mortgage and therefore no mortgage interest or investment interest to deduct. They donated $12,000 a year to charity. This left them with only $22,000 in itemized deductions, which makes opting for their combined $24,000 standard deduction the best choice, even though they benefited significantly in prior years from the deductibility of their large state, local, and real estate taxes.

Under the new tax code, there would be no tax reduction benefit in donating $12,000 a year to charity because, combined with the $10,000 cap on state, local, and real estate taxes, it would fall below the standard allowance and effectively be filtered out. However, one strategy that helped them get above the standard deduction threshold is to bundle two years' donations into one. For example, if they donate $12,000 a year, they can donate $24,000 in one year and combine this deduction with their $10,000 state, local, and real estate allowance to itemize $34,000 in total deductions in one year, which will lower their tax bill. The second year, they would make no charitable contribution but take the standard deduction. Reviewing any areas that can be bundled to benefit from itemizing deductions is a good strategy in any individual's financial plan.

You may qualify for special deductions that can have significant benefits from a tax-planning perspective. These special deductions may include college and educational items, student loan interest, and educator expenses. These are not large deductions and don't apply to everybody, but they are some of the items that every good tax-planning expert should look for from a higher-level tax-planning preparation standpoint to help reduce a client's tax burden.

Credits

A credit is usually more beneficial to the client than a deduction. A deduction reduces taxable income, which means the tax savings will be a percentage of the dollars that were spent on the deductible expense. For example, a $1,000 deduction for someone in the 30 percent tax bracket will yield a $300 reduction in tax liability. However, a credit is usually a dollar-for-dollar savings. For example, a $1,000 tax credit reduces the tax liability by $1,000.

Sitting down with a tax specialist to discuss possible credits is always advisable, as these vary greatly from client to client. For example, a client with children may qualify for a child credit. There may be tax benefits to paying a household employee for childcare versus taking a credit for daycare. These decisions are part of the lifestyle allowances that every tax preparer should consider for every client.

There may be credits available from a flexible spending account (FSA) or a health savings account (HSA). These accounts are two types of employee benefits designed to save employees money through pretax savings on eligible healthcare expenses. The FSA is one of several tax-advantaged financial accounts that offer payroll tax savings. The most common type of FSA is used to pay for medical and dental expenses not covered by insurance, including deductibles, copayments, and coinsurance for the employee's health plan. Since the Affordable Care Act came into effect in 2010, up to $500 of funds in the FSA can be transferred from one year to the next. The HSA is a tax-advantaged medical savings account. The funds contributed to an account are not subject to federal income tax at the time of deposit and accumulate year to year if they are not spent. A tax specialist can review a client's accounts to determine whether some expenses, including childcare expenses, can be put through an FSA without incurring a tax liability.

Other tax credits exist for those who invest in energy-saving additions to their house, such as doors, windows, furnaces, air conditioning units, or geothermal units. College credits exist for parents who are paying their children's tuition and college expenses. Retirement income credits and elderly credits can apply to many clients.

One benefit of forward planning is that it offers the ability to identify in advance where there is a potential tax savings in the timing of decisions, bundling deductions, and understanding what credits may be available to offset decisions throughout the year. This effective forward planning is predicated on a good client–tax specialist relationship and ongoing communication.

RETIREMENT PLANNING

While the most common concern people have when it comes to taxes is reducing or deferring them, the next area of concern usually relates to retirement planning.

Most people are concerned about planning for retirement and adopting efficient tax strategies to support that goal. Both old and new tax codes encourage people to put money into their company 401(k) and defer paying taxes on that money until they retire. Most employers offer a matching program for their company's 401(k) plan, typically matching an employee's contribution fifty cents per dollar, and sometimes dollar for dollar, up to the first 6 percent of the person's earnings. Taxes are not owed at the time income is placed in the 401(k), making this a good tax-planning strategy. The pretax deferment is efficient, as it is based on the expectation that an employee will be in a lower tax bracket when they retire. Additional advantages of paying into a 401(k) include benefiting from compounding interest or growth on both the employee's deposit and the employer's match throughout the employee's working life.

The employer's match is additional or bonus income. Thus, when employees decide not to participate in a 401(k), they are not only missing out on the tax deferment; they are also giving up that bonus income from the employer match. From a tax planning as well as an investment planning perspective, this employee is losing out at a time when saving for retirement is crucial. Putting 6 percent of income away to maximize the company match is a significant help toward building a good retirement source of income.

Those planning for retirement need to be aware of alternate tax strategies. For example, many baby boomers have reached retirement age and are receiving distributions from their retirement plans. However, because of the financial downturn, many of them needed to take early distributions (before age fifty-nine) from their IRA and 401(k) plans. As a result, they incurred a 10 percent premature distribution penalty. This was only exempted in cases of financial hardship or health issues, but many baby boomers were not even aware of this exemption.

This situation again points to the necessity of having a good client–tax specialist relationship that involves ongoing dialogue so that the challenges facing the former can be addressed by the latter to ensure tax penalties are not incurred with the early distribution for a necessity.

Other people wait until they are age seventy-two, when they are required to take money out of their IRA. But with proper tax planning, they may not have to wait that long. If they are in a low tax bracket, they might consider taking social security because there will be no (or very little) income tax ramifications from doing so. Therefore, regardless of circumstances, retirees wondering when they should begin drawing from social security or withdrawing money from their retirement funds should first discuss the tax implications with their tax planner.

While the expertise in any tax plan lies with the tax planner, tax awareness on the part of the client is a key to a solid forward approach. A good tax expert will take responsibility for educating clients by offering seminars, newsletters, and tax information so that clients are educated enough about taxation to know what questions to raise or what issues necessitate calling their tax specialist. Before engaging any tax specialist, it is advisable to inquire whether they offer these benefits. From there, it is important to check that there is good communication between team members to ensure that an overall healthy financial plan is designed that can withstand and adjust to the normal challenges and changing events in a person's life.

Here's what I tell my clients, and I want to share it with you. You have a choice to make: You can make your heirs the sole beneficiaries of your estate, or you can make the federal government and your heirs *joint beneficiaries*! If you craft things properly, you can allow the money you worked so hard for to grow and ultimately pass on what you don't spend to your heirs. You get to choose—as long as you plan ahead!

TAKEAWAY

→ The tax planner is a key member of any financial planning team, and tax planning should always be approached by looking forward and not by looking in the rearview mirror.

→ This requires having open communication between team members so that tax implications can be assessed when changes occur in life circumstances or before making key decisions, such as getting a bonus, exercising a stock option, losing a job, getting married, or buying or refinancing a home.

→ A good financial planner will have a partner in a CPA firm to help support clients' tax needs. Before engaging a financial planner, you should assess whether he or she gets involved in the income tax aspects of a client's wealth-management plan. If so, to what extent?

Investment planning can never be done in a vacuum because investment decisions always have tax implications. To avoid upsetting surprises at tax time, it is important that the tax plan be viewed along with all other aspects of a wealth-management plan, so that the tax picture a client will face at the end of the year can be viewed in advance—not during tax season when it's too late to make changes.

The main takeaway from this chapter—what I want my clients and you to always keep in mind—is this: considering tax law changes, it is important that you do tax projections in advance to determine if there are any strategies to shift expenses or income from one year to another to play the tax game the right way. Even though you may have read or heard that we have simplified income taxes, the truth is it's as complex as ever, and working with a financial advisor and a tax professional as a team can minimize your taxes and help you keep more of what you worked hard to earn.

I hope you benefited from this peek behind the curtain of tax planning. In the next chapter, we are going to take the same approach to investment management.

CHAPTER 11

Pulling Back the Curtain on Investment Management

An integral part of any financial plan is the investment in and management of different securities and other assets in order to meet your specific investment goals. The key is having a clear understanding of both how to do it as well as who should be helping you. In this chapter, we will delve into this area based on my forty-plus years of experience. We will also discuss the dos and don'ts by pulling the curtain back so that you can see what Oz really looks like.

Forty or fifty years ago, the trend was to invest in individual securities (i.e., stocks and bonds), and this continued through the tech boom of the mid- to late 1990s. Even today, many people still hold individual securities. Oftentimes, they own shares in the company for which they work. Although these may play a role in a portfolio, based on my experience, a better investment building block today is the use of a variety of actively managed mutual funds, which combines stocks and bonds from a variety of individual companies into a single investment fund. Mutual fund companies assemble these individual securities into different mutual funds, each of which will have its own approach and objectives in terms of how it invests money. This means that whether an individual is investing his or her own money or working with a financial planner, the objectives of funds in the portfolio should align with the client's goals and risk temperament. For example, depending on the individual's needs, timeline, and risk tolerance, the individual can choose funds that are more growth oriented or income oriented.

ACTIVE MANAGEMENT

In addition to an individual's investment goals, you should consider many other factors before investing in a mutual fund, including who is managing the fund, the fund's benchmarks and stock turnover, fees and costs, and whether the fund is actively or passively managed. Today, there is a prevailing argument that passively managed funds—that is "buying index funds or ETFs"—is the ideal approach to investing rather than buying into mutual funds that are actively managed by an individual fund manager or a team of portfolio managers.

At Chornyak & Associates, we subscribe to the philosophy that the best way to properly manage risk and earn returns that are similar to the market is through active management. Our philosophy when it comes to helping people select mutual fund investments is predicated on the extensive analysis and studies similar to those that have been done by Steve Deschenes, director of product management and analytics at the Capital Group, home of American Funds®, a family of mutual funds that have different goals and objectives but are all marketed and administered under the Capital Group name. Each mutual fund in the American Funds family is actively managed and has a set of objectives in terms of how it invests people's money.

I'm honored to have worked with them since 1984, and they are the largest mutual fund firm that we have used over the years. The reasons are consistency and their philosophy of doing what is best for clients, controlling expenses, and having a long-term view. Just as important, they put significant amounts of their own money into the funds that they manage, so they have significant skin in the game. Their philosophy aligns so closely with how we have built our firm that I see it as one of the best investment firms, bar none, and I feel fortunate to have come across it when I did so many years ago. Having collaborated about investments with Steve over the years, I hoped he would be willing to share his thoughts based on some of the studies they've done, and I'm grateful he agreed to having their voice be part of this chapter.

In this chapter, we will look at why active management is important. We will also address other key issues every individual should consider before investing in a mutual fund, from knowing what to look for in terms of fund performance, what questions to ask a fund manager, what time frame considerations and objectives need to be factored into decisions, and how to spot red flags.

WHAT OZ REALLY LOOKS LIKE

I have been a believer my entire career that it is important as an advisor to know the portfolio managers, analysts, and researchers that are managing my money—and my clients' money. I have always made it a point to go to conferences to which I've been invited and meet the people who are actually managing my clients' money. I want to look at them, eyeball to eyeball, hear the inflection of their voices, and watch their body language to see how passionate and committed they are. Or are not.

In the 1980s, I was privileged to meet Sir John Templeton, the American-born British investment banker, fund manager, and philanthropist known back then as the "Father of Mutual Funds." Over the years, I have also been honored to meet (on multiple occasions) with many of the most respected portfolio managers in the country with Capital Group/American Funds, MFS, Franklin Templeton, and Fidelity, to name just a few.

Over the decades, I have been able to do something the consumer cannot do. I attend meetings regularly and have breakfast, lunch, and dinner with some of the best portfolio managers in the country. Because of that, I can pull back that curtain to see what Oz really looks like. Before I invest my money or anyone else's, I have to have a comfort level in my gut. Over the years, I've been invited to numerous conferences and heard hundreds of portfolio managers. Here's what I've learned.

THE DOG AND PONY SHOW

I was invited in the early 1990s to a two-day by-invitation-only conference in Houston with a high-flying mutual fund company. I had not used that family of mutual funds before and was interested in getting a better understanding of how they invested as well as the opportunity to meet with the portfolio managers.

Picture this. I'm there with probably fifty or sixty other advisors in a room. They bring in different portfolio managers to make presentations and answer questions. After lunch, we're going to hear a hotshot portfolio manager with an incredible track record. Right before that, I went to the restroom, where I overheard two gentlemen talking. They weren't aware I had entered, too engrossed in their conversation to notice.

"Ready to speak?" one of them asked the other.

"Yes," the other one replied. "Let's get this dog and pony show on the road again. We'll tell them what they want to hear."

They both chuckled, and then they left.

I went back to the conference room and watched as they introduced the hotshot portfolio manager. When I heard his voice, I knew he was the one who was chuckling and describing this presentation as a dog and pony show.

I asked a question, and Mr. Hotshot dodged it. His presentation was very salesy, and he dodged a variety of questions from others as well. I never felt comfortable with the fund, or the fund company, and we never used any of the funds in that fund family. As the market became more volatile, this particular fund got beat up severely. It doesn't happen that often, but if you meet a portfolio manager, and you aren't comfortable with the answers that you're getting to your questions, then maybe there's a reason not to use that mutual fund. I've learned over the years to follow my gut and instincts. It's helped me dodge a number of bullets.

BUILT ON TRUST

The point is, when you have a small group of advisors, and you can ask pointed questions and see the responses, it gives you a feeling of whether they will do what's right. When we invest money, it's all built on trust. Our clients trust us with their financial lives, and we don't take that lightly. It's important for me to trust the portfolio managers and analysts the way my clients trust me.

Here's something a lot of people don't think about very often, something you need to be aware of. Trust is based on relationships, not track records. I

> Trust is based on relationships, not track records.

can't tell you how many funds out there today have historic track records that don't mean very much to me because the team is entirely different than the one who created that historic track record. That's one of the reasons I reached out to Capital Group/American Funds for the team members to share directly with you some of their research. It's the kind of research that I've used my entire career, and it's allowed us to select which mutual funds we should use to build a well-diversified portfolio for our clients.

Next, we will share some of the biggest mistakes people make when it comes to investment selection and management.

5 COMMON INVESTMENT MISTAKES

- A big mistake people who do not work with an advisor make is getting into the market toward the end of a bull market. This results in their buying high and selling low. Most people do not have the risk profile to do as Warren Buffet says, "Buy when others are fearful, and sell when others are greedy." This is a good argument for why working with a seasoned advisor and diversifying among a variety of professional fund managers is effective at mitigating some of people's inherent behavioral biases, including the tendency to overreact to short-term input.

- The second mistake people make is investing in passively managed index funds and exchange traded funds (ETFs). Because the US equity markets have done very well since the financial meltdown that ended March 9, 2009, an attitude developed in the investing public that it is a good idea to go out and buy an ETF or a passively managed index fund that mirrors the S&P 500 based on its rate of return. In the next section, we will look at why this approach creates risk—a risk that most people don't realize!

- Another mistake people make when investing in mutual funds is failing to understand the qualities that indicate excellence in an investment company and its fund managers, including corporate culture, attracting and retaining fund managers, teamwork, portfolio turnover or stock rotation, and global flexibility. These qualities differentiate both the fund managers and the funds themselves from the broad markets. We will examine this in more detail later in this chapter.

- A fourth mistake people make when investing in mutual funds is chasing fads rather than understanding market cycles and the hazards of rapid stock rotation. They end up buying into a fund based on its performance the previous year without looking at the historic returns or changes in the underlying value of the company stocks within the fund. Related to this is a focus on rate of return without looking at how much risk was taken to get that return and the total fees that are being charged, or without having a clear understanding of who is managing the fund and whether this person has his or her own money invested in that fund.

- The fifth mistake people make is failing to factor in their own time horizons—that is, when the money will be needed. If someone needs money back in fewer than three years, it is not long-term investment money, at least not money that should be invested in the stock market. We will look at why these are important issues later in this chapter.

WORKING WITH AN ADVISOR

In general, working with a seasoned professional advisor to invest in mutual funds is the ideal way to avoid common mistakes. The majority of individuals is not able to devote the time and energy to do enough in-depth research to become expert enough to manage investments effectively on their own. Most people want to spend time with their families or engage in activities that they enjoy. They generally don't want to spend their weekends doing exhaustive research on Morningstar and reading the *Wall Street Journal* and *Barron's*. The best course, therefore, is to work with someone who does.

For example, the Capital Group's Growth Fund of America has twelve portfolio managers who work with seventy or eighty analysts in individual sectors. One is an expert in the pharmaceutical industry and does deep research into clinical trials and the pharmaceutical pipeline. This person understands the management team of a company and where capital is being allocated—for example, into growth initiatives. This analyst provides a report on the company, its management team, and its expectations for future earnings. This information is then passed along to the portfolio managers, who make investment decisions based on that analyst's report and recommendations. In other words, with hundreds of people who are highly compensated and highly skilled, the group has a complex and extensive process for researching, analyzing, and choosing securities. Fortunately, because they are managing a lot of money, they can distribute their fixed costs across lots of investors and keep costs low.

Another reason I recommend working with an advisor is that he or she can evaluate how much risk a client should be taking, not necessarily how much they want to take, in the context of their overall financial circumstances. This is why we first strive to understand what assets our clients have, how much money they have available, and when they need that money. This financial picture determines how much risk they can afford to take (not necessarily how much risk they want to take) and whether they should be in long-term or short-term investments. That, in turn, drives the process of narrowing the focus to identify the right mutual funds and investment buckets that are available in the marketplace today. Portfolios need to be segmented between cash reserves and long-term investments based on timelines and risk temperament. This ensures that money that will be needed in six months or a year from now is not invested in the stock market because this runs the risk of pulling money out of one's investments when the market is down. We will look at time frames in more detail later in this chapter.

Once a financial advisor has established the parameters of a client's assets and goals, he or she is then positioned to work with different fund families. At Chornyak & Associates, we use a variety of mutual funds and fund families that meet our rigid criteria, including the Capital Group's American Funds, which most closely align with the risk temperament and diversification needs of our clients.

ACTIVE VERSUS PASSIVE MANAGEMENT

Active versus passive management is a contested issue. There is a school of investors and advisors who think that markets are efficient and therefore cannot be beaten. This school believes in the efficient market hypothesis, which was first espoused by Burton Malkiel,[1] and the capital asset pricing model proposed by Bill Sharpe and Harry Markowitz, which essentially says that all the information that is available about a stock is already priced into that stock, and there is

---

1   Burton Malkiel, *A Random Walk down Wall Street* (New York: W. W. Norton & Company, 1973).

no gain to be made by either buying or selling it. The result of these theories is the belief that markets are efficient and outperforming them is difficult. The best strategy therefore is to just let the market do what the market does, which is grow over time.

However, markets are not purely efficient, and an investor or fund manager can gain an advantage by taking an active role, doing some research and investment analysis, and meeting with companies and their senior management to help make more informed choices. This will be reflected in a return that is potentially better than the return from a passively managed portfolio.

The Capital Group has consistently shown active management to produce these results.[2] It conducted research back to 1931 and, using a month as a unit of return, looked at every rolling one-, three-, five-, ten-, fifteen-, twenty-, twenty-five-, and thirty-year period. From this data, they asked how often a group of managers beat the index and by how much they beat it. In other words, was their win big enough to justify the risk they took? By looking backward, the group was able to assess historic factors and project forward over the next ten years to build a better predictive model that would allow them not to track the market but to beat it.

Over the last eighty years, the group has produced 150 to 200 basis points, or 1.5–2 percent, above the market. Therefore, while markets may be efficient, they are not so efficient that an advantage cannot be gained through active management that will help a client achieve their investment goals with a greater degree of success.

It is important, therefore, that before choosing a fund, an investor look at the long sweep of history and at more fundamental,

---

2   For more information, see Robin Wigglesworth and Stephen Foley, "Capital Group takes on the passive investors," *Financial Times*, March 20, 2017, https://www.ft.com/content/5e1df770-0d58-11e7-a88c-50ba212dce4d.

consistent, and durable factors—or work with a financial planner or fund managers who do.

CHARACTERISTICS OF GOOD FUND MANAGEMENT

Statistics show that it is possible to outperform the market by being active and adopting a differentiating approach. This approach is multifaceted and requires attracting the right people who exhibit the characteristics every investor should look for in a fund manager.

Any successful fund management company will know how to create a culture where managers are invested in the company itself; how to identify, attract, and keep the right people without compromising the client's returns; how to structure a team to manage a fund; and how to achieve success by taking a flexible approach to global securities.

Corporate Culture

Often, publicly traded investment companies focus on attracting very smart people, after which their focus becomes holding onto them over the long term through the star system, the compensation structure, how they recruit, and how they think about managing people. Then, in addition to paying portfolio managers, the firm must pay shareholders, which creates upward pressure on the internal mutual fund fees.

Private companies, such as the Capital Group, on the other hand, created a corporate and investment culture that invests in the investors. It aligns portfolio management compensation with a bonus structure that is based on performance over multiple time periods and also with ownership in the firm because the shareholders are the portfolio managers. This gives fund managers a natural incentive to keep the company strong, which means the objectives of the company and the fund managers are aligned. This is part of the reason why the Capital Group has been so successful and why individual investors should work with a financial planner who has built a long-standing relationship with fund companies whose philosophy is to increase the wealth of their clients.

Identifying Good Managers

In addition to the benefits gained from working with a private company, the process of hiring and retaining fund managers is crucial to the success of any fund.

For example, the Capital Group undertook considerable research to identify the important factors to look for in an investment manager. They went to their largest plan sponsors, clients, consultants, and advisors and asked a series of questions:

- How do you choose an investment manager?

- What are the things that matter to you?

- What factors are incorporated into that choice?

Then they asked: How do you know that your factors are adding value? How do you hold yourself accountable that those factors are producing the results you're looking for?

From these answers, they built a predictive model that could help select mutual funds that had a go-forward approach and would produce a portfolio that would do better than the market. The bottom line was that the company was able to identify factors that helped them choose the mutual funds that were more likely to do better than the market. These factors were surprisingly intuitive, straightforward, and accessible to any investor trying to pick a mutual fund in which to invest.

The five factors any investor should look at in a mutual fund are these:

- Cost or fees

- Ownership of funds

- Compensation

- Manager volatility

- Team structure

COST STRUCTURE

The first step to finding a good mutual fund is to ignore the top three-quarters of the most expensive funds in terms of their internal fund expenses and focus instead on the least expensive quartile. Portfolio managers add value in general before fees and expenses. Most actively managed mutual funds charge too much, and therefore, whatever value they create is eroded by fees and internal expenses, so that the net value they add for an investor becomes negative. Therefore, investors who seek out low-cost mutual funds who have the scale, the stewardship, and the culture to consistently lower their internal fees when their scale allows typically do dramatically better.

OWNERSHIP

The second step is to choose mutual funds where the managers who are managing the fund have a significant amount of their own money invested in the fund that they manage. By significant, I mean at least $1 million of their own money. If a fund manager is not invested in his own funds, then neither should individual investors. Otherwise, it would be like eating in a restaurant where the chef will not eat.

The Capital Group did an exhaustive study of the universe of mutual funds, took the quartile of managers who had the most money invested in their own funds, combined that with the quartile of mutual funds with the lowest internal fund expenses and fees, and was able to identify the best low-cost, high-manager ownership. Further analysis then showed that those mutual funds did consistently better than the broad market index in every time period they examined and in every asset class that they analyzed by a meaningful amount.

COMPENSATION

A third step is looking at how managers are compensated. At the Capital Group, managers are paid a bonus based on one-, three-, five-, and eight-year periods of rolling returns. Rolling returns are annualized average returns for a period that highlight the funds' stronger and poorer periods of performance. Rolling returns can offer better insight into a fund's more comprehensive return history, rather than just its most recent data. For fund managers at American Funds, the longer the timeline for those rolling periods, the bigger the bonus at the end of the period. This encourages a long-term focus rather than making a quick hit.

VOLATILITY

A fourth step is to look at manager volatility. If a mutual fund changes managers, and the new manager has a different focus, then it is no longer the same fund. However, a fund such as the Growth Fund of America is composed of twelve managers, each managing 5 to 10 percent of the portfolio. The advantage here is that if one manager retires, that 10 percent of the portfolio can be distributed among the other eleven managers until another manager is added. This makes for a smoother transitioning experience. This is different from many investment funds today, where high management turnover results in big changes in the underlying fund. This is especially true where, with some fund companies, there is a single star portfolio manager managing the mutual fund. Long-term consistency in management and philosophy is paramount in a fund and fund manager.

TEAMWORK

While some people may make better managers than others, one manager is not better all the time in all markets. Investors stand to benefit from investing in funds managed by a team. For example, one manager may be very growth oriented and always on the lookout for the next best stock, which means they are less concerned about income and dividends. If this person is managing a fund alone, he or she is exposed to vicissitudes of how this fund will

> Investors stand to benefit from investing in funds managed by a team.

appreciate or not in the broader market. Conversely, with a team approach, some managers will be a little more conservative and focus on dividend-oriented stocks. On their own, they may rein themselves in more if their stock holdings constitute their entire portfolio (or the client's entire portfolio), but as part of a team, growth managers have more freedom, and conservative managers bring balance, so that overall, the fund performs effectively in the long term.

Global Flexibility

Many investment companies overlook the importance of adding global securities to their family of funds. At first glance, this may not seem unusual considering that US securities outperformed the ex-US Securities over the last ten years. However, thirty of the top fifty securities over the last ten years have been outside the United States. Therefore, while ex-US markets overall haven't done well, individual companies have done exceedingly well. A firm that has the flexibility and global research support to identify those companies and pass on these benefits to investors is an important characteristic to support any long-term portfolio growth.

STOCK ROTATION AND RATE OF RETURN

Warren Buffet has quoted his mentor Benjamin Graham as saying, "In the short run, the market is a voting machine—reflecting a voter-registration test that requires only money, not intelligence or emotional stability—but in the long run, the market is a weighing machine."[3] This is consistent with Graham's 1934 book, *Security Analysis*, in which he tells a post–Great Depression cautionary tale about not following market fads. In the short term, the market behaves like a popularity contest, with stock prices changing rapidly, even though the underlying true value of the companies doesn't change. However, when measured over multiple business cycles, the biases that affect the market fade, and the true value of a company, based on metrics such as cash flow, return on investment, and earnings, remains.

Because biases and fads obscure the true value of a stock in the short term, try to avoid looking at the rate of return of a fund in the short term, especially while overlooking how much risk was taken to get that rate of return or without having a clear understanding of who is managing the fund and whether this person has his or her own money invested in the fund.

Markets have exploitable inefficiencies, but less so in the short term, which means short-term differentiation from the broad market is harder to achieve. The industry average turnover of stocks within a fund is usually between twelve and twenty-four months. That means within one or two years the fund has 100 percent portfolio turnover.

---

3   The quote was attributed to Ben Graham by Warren Buffett in the 1993 Berkshire Hathaway letter to shareholders.

The turnover in funds at the Capital Group is three to four years on average, and some last for ten years or more. The portfolio managers at American Funds believe in investing in high-quality companies for the long term and do not let short-term volatility sway owning these companies. This lower turnover offsets short-term market inefficiencies.

In addition, the longer the stocks inside the fund are held, the more insights are garnered that can identify something that will change the earnings capacity of a company. If that is identified in advance, then the fund can benefit before the rest of the market catches up.

For any investor interested in investing in a mutual fund, it is advisable that they look at mutual fund companies that adopt this long view and can show strong fund performance over a ten-year rolling period compared to the traditional short-term benchmarks against which funds are measured.

RISK AND TIME HORIZONS

Sometimes, investors will look at their 401(k)s and not like the performance they see in a mutual fund. It may be that the fund has not done well over the previous couple of years. However, you should always look at rolling periods and fund performance across market cycles. Anyone invested in the stock market should be willing to leave their money in place for seven to ten years or more. If they need their money in two to three years, they should not be in the stock market but in shorter-term securities, treasuries, and other products that have very little possibility of declining significantly.

Evaluating fund performance in longer time frames is even more important for people who have long-term retirement goals and want to leave a legacy for their children. This is another reason it is important that each client's portfolio contain funds that are aligned with the individual investor's objectives across market cycles and across life cycles. People's objectives change. At twenty-five, you will be more growth focused and less concerned about the downside. At sixty-five, when your money needs to be drawn for retirement, your primary consideration in your portfolio is probably going to be preservation of capital and your dividend yield.

In the retirement stage, there should be some changes in the types of equities in which you invest. A seasoned financial planner should be able to shift the retiree's investment away from those with riskier downside characteristics. This means sitting with a financial planner to identify shifting goals is a crucial part of the financial planning and wealth-management process.

TAKEAWAY

There are many benefits of investing in actively managed mutual funds: They are managed professionally, which gives the investor expertise without having to track the fund performance themselves. There are tremendous scale advantages to be gained. And it is easier to put together a reasonable portfolio of mutual funds by working with an advisor.

Before investing in a fund, it is important to ask a financial planner about the objectives of that particular fund:

➔ What is the primary objective of the fund?

➔ Is the fund about growth and capital appreciation or preservation or income? (If a fund is focused on income, it will comprise securities that are more stable, have a higher dividend yield, and be more focused on producing the income for the investor.)

➔ Are there dividend-paying stocks in the portfolio?

➔ What kind of portfolio turnover is there inside that particular fund?

➔ How long has the portfolio management team been managing the fund?

➔ Do the managers of the fund have significant skin in the game by having their own money invested in the fund that they manage?

➔ How has this fund done compared to the benchmarks that it's measured against?

➔ Does the financial planner have any of his or her money in the recommended fund?

Not only will the answers to these questions offer guidance about the suitability of a fund, but they will expose the skill and knowledge of the financial advisor. Many people in the financial services industry claim to be advisors when, in reality, they are salespeople who are not offering a true service oriented toward doing what's best for the client in the long run.

This is another reason why it is very important to assess the value of advice when working with an advisor. This is not limited to advice on investment return but also how much hand holding, behavioral coaching, and saving advice is involved. A good investment advisor will remind you of strategies you can adopt to increase your wealth—for example, exploring the idea of converting some of your existing IRA to a Roth IRA and using that as an opportunity to do some helpful tax planning.

Ultimately, investment management, financial planning, and tax planning are interdependent. A successful financial strategy will factor these various mechanisms into an overall plan to offer you better investment options. Done well, a lifestyle of choice can be created that offers options to work or not to work and spend time with family and to be able to leave a legacy without worrying about outliving money. That is the true value of advice.

Here is my ultimate takeaway. In my forty years of doing what I do, I think it's extremely important to be properly diversified, be careful in the selection of the underlying investments or mutual funds, be patient, and don't let your emotions get in the way of your long-term goals and objectives. Finally, don't base investment decisions primarily on rate of return but rather on long-term objectives of a particular mutual fund and the quality and longevity of the portfolio managers of each fund. Make sure that those managers have significant skin in the game—that is, at least $1 million of their own money in the fund that they manage.

Next is something many of us would like to put off but that you must deal with to make sure these decisions are made by you and not someone else.

CHAPTER 12

How to Do Estate Planning

Y ou see the advertisements everywhere: Do it yourself. Make your own will. Create an online trust.

I have one thing to say about all those ads and what they're asking of you. *Don't do it!*

YOU'RE SMART; THAT'S NOT THE ISSUE

Of course, you're smart enough to do your own estate planning. That's not the point I'm trying to make here. It's not a question of whether you're smart enough. But estate planning is not what you do naturally. I'm sure that I could get a book and figure out how to repair my car or how to put a filling in my tooth, but is that what I want to do? Is that my area of expertise? How can you do what you do best and what I do best at the same time?

During the COVID-19 quarantine, people took on many jobs they had previously entrusted to experts. One day, I ran into an attorney with whom we work, and something was different about him—something not good.

"Did you get a haircut?" I asked.

"I tried cutting it myself, and I screwed it up," he said with an embarrassed grin. "And I shaved it all off."

If you screw up your hair, it will grow back. If you screw up the money you amassed and accumulated, you may not have enough years to get it all back. Cutting your hair isn't a life-altering event. COVID-19 is live altering. The financial meltdown of 2008 was life altering. Many people left a bunch of money on the table because they let their emotions get in the way of common sense. That money you leave on the table won't grow back as quickly as your hair.

A married couple came to our office recently to create a financial plan. They had investment accounts, retirement accounts, and savings accounts, along with property and other valuables, yet they had done no estate planning. Like many people, they believed that because the value of their estate did not exceed the federal inheritance tax exemption of over $11 million per individual, estate planning wasn't necessary. However, having reviewed their assets, I realized that not only did they need a will, but they needed a trust. We'll look at the difference between wills and trusts later in this chapter.

The first issue facing the couple was that many of their accounts were not titled properly. That is, they had not named a contingent beneficiary on their life insurance and retirement funds, which meant that these accounts would end up going through the lengthy and expensive probate process if they happened to both pass away quickly. They also had an unmarried son, who had started up a risky business and had a number of creditors. If they died, and their son inherited their estate directly through their will, the inherited assets wouldn't be protected from creditors since they had not set up a trust. Nor could they prevent him from investing what assets remained in another risky venture. Neither had the couple established a financial or medical power of attorney or an end-of-life directive.

In our first meeting, they realized that there was far more to estate planning than just making a will and assuming their assets would go to their son, including potential issues with how the surviving partner would carry out end-of-life wishes for the other and whether their son understood their wishes for their personal belongings and their financial assets should the decision-making responsibility fall to him.

With every financial plan we design for clients at Chornyak & Associates, we work through all aspects of an estate plan. We then refer clients to meet with an attorney with Pappas Gibson LLC, an exceptional estate planning law firm in Columbus, Ohio, with whom we have worked for more than thirty years. Estate planning is about 50 percent of the firm's practice; the other half is focused on business and real estate. At Pappas Gibson, Bob Pappas or Matt Gibson usually meets with our clients and prepares estate planning documents: the will, trust, financial power of attorney, medical power of attorney, and living will. Once these legal documents are in place and reflect a client's wishes, we continue to work in tandem with Bob and Matt to make sure the estate plan is kept up to date and reflects ongoing changes in our clients' lives and their assets.

Bob and Matt are two of the brightest attorneys I know—very practical, honest, and fair. To put it more bluntly, if I got hit by that proverbial bus today, Bob is actually a cotrustee of all that I have with my son. As we are formulating a plan, asking all the questions we ask, we get Bob and Matt involved to look at all the client's agreements, wills, trusts, and powers of attorney. They help us put together an outline to bring estate planning documents up to date. Some are twenty—or more—years old. Ask yourself when was the last time you updated your estate planning documents. The world is different today, and the estate tax laws are different.

In the past, we put money into trusts to avoid paying estate taxes too soon. Today, estate planning is more designed to protect your estate from creditors, divorce, or business failures. It is extremely important to take what people have today and make sure it passes to their children, grandchildren, and great-grandchildren as well as to create a legacy that doesn't get squandered. Having updated wills and trusts and medical and financial powers of attorney is critical. Equally critical is making sure assets you now own are properly owned and titled in such a manner that you can minimize and many times avoid probate. Many attorneys consider probate their friend because it allows them to charge legal fees to those who must go through probate.

> Having updated wills and trusts and medical and financial powers of attorney is critical.

IMPORTANT CONSIDERATIONS

When considering what would or could happen after your death, you may not have thought about all the possibilities. It's important, if you have children from various marriages, that both parents and stepparents have a medical power of attorney on the children and stepchildren.

Suppose you are a stepparent watching a minor child. Suppose again that your stepchild is injured. You cannot make medical decisions unless you have a medical power of attorney for that child.

Now, suppose your children have reached majority. Perhaps they're in college or on their first jobs. They're now adults, and you'd better have a medical power of attorney and a financial power of attorney on your adult children, so that you can make medical and financial decisions for these newly adult children.

These are simple, straightforward documents. You also need a medical or a legal power of attorney between you and your spouse. Suppose the husband amasses a bunch of money in a 401(k) or an IRA and is still alive but incapacitated. His wife cannot make changes to the 401(k) or IRA without the power of attorney while the husband is alive because it's not hers.

You should review your documents and update them, if necessary, every four to five years. If you don't, and if something happens to you, the financial institutions might question whether those documents are still valid because they are stale.

WHAT IS AN ESTATE PLAN?

Many people think that once they write a will, they've finished their estate planning, but this is far from the case. Every estate plan has two components. The first, called the lifetime planning component, sets out a person's wishes for their personal and their financial assets while they are alive. The second addresses what they want to happen to their assets after they die. This is handled by wills and trusts. Let's take a close look at each component.

ESTATE PLAN COMPONENT ONE—
LIFETIME PLANNING

The life planning component of an estate plan takes care of the clients and their assets during their lifetime. This is primarily handled by assigning financial and medical powers of attorney and other advanced directives to an individual or individuals of choice and possibly creating a living will.

Financial Power of Attorney

The financial power of attorney directs what should happen when clients are unable to make financial decisions. It names someone to act on their behalf in the event they are not able to act for themselves. Appointing a financial power of attorney is not naming an attorney, or an accountant, or a financial advisor. It names somebody to whom the client is personally related, associated, or comfortable with. It can be a parent, sibling, spouse, child, or friend. Before you make that choice, you should ask yourself, "If something happened to me, is this the person I would like to step in my shoes because I know that they will have my best interests at heart, and that they will do the right thing, and they won't ignore my wishes or steal the money from me?" It is recommended that the person chosen can be trusted to do what the client would do were he or she able to make decisions for him or herself.

Because the person who is assigned the power of attorney will have the ability to step in and assume control over all financial affairs, there is considerable trust involved in this arrangement. The person will effectively have control over the client's checkbook. They can make sure bills are paid and income checks are deposited. They will work with the client's financial advisor to keep investments on track and implement necessary changes. Therefore, it is important that they be capable of handling this role.

Beyond these responsibilities, this person will have some control over how the client lives. For example, if someone is incapacitated but wants to stay at home for the rest of his or her life, regardless of the cost, a financial power of attorney will need to be assigned to someone who will be capable of authorizing those expenses to make that happen for them. If a different person holds the medical power of attorney, these two wishes could be at odds.

For example, while end-of-life housing wishes can be stipulated in the power of attorney document, it is important to remember that circumstances can change. Staying at home could be dangerous for someone's health in addition to a drain on their finances. Therefore, it may be better that the person who is assigned the financial power of attorney be given discretion to change the client's wishes as the situation demands.

If there is no one trustworthy or knowledgeable enough available to handle a person's business affairs, a financial planner can recommend that you create a trust. Pappas Gibson has set up trusts for our clients in a way that they name a professional trust company as the trustee. The trust then handles the accounting, and we continue to handle the investment decisions within the trust on the client's behalf. Usually, Bob and Matt work with clients to set up a directive if they want Chornyak & Associates to handle their financial affairs if they become incapacitated. We can then take care of their assets rather than leave them in the hands of someone not qualified or reliable enough to manage them for them.

TYPES OF POWERS OF ATTORNEY

There are two different types of power of attorney available, depending on the needs or situation: a general power of attorney and a springing power of attorney.

Once signed, a general power of attorney is always in effect, giving the person named control over all the client's financial affairs. This document is a longer-term document, not something to be signed because, for example, someone is buying a piece of property and needs someone to step in for the closing because they are on vacation.

A springing power of attorney is similar to a general power of attorney, but it has restrictions. Most commonly, the restriction will stipulate that the document remain dormant until an event makes it "spring" to life. An estate attorney would add a paragraph to the springing power of attorney stipulating that if a particular event occurs—for example, the client becomes incapacitated and cannot make medical decisions on their own behalf—two physicians could sign statements confirming the client cannot make financial decisions on their own behalf because of a medical condition. These two statements will effectively serve to spring the power of attorney document into life and allow the person named in it to make financial decisions on the client's behalf for the duration of his or her incapacitation.

A Medical Power of Attorney

A medical power of attorney specifies who should make medical decisions in the event someone is incapacitated and unable to make those decisions themselves.

This document is designed so that, should a client be unable to make medical decisions on their own behalf, the person or persons named have the power to do so for them. These people are usually family members because they are emotionally involved with the client's well-being and are also the people who are interfacing with medical staff. Giving them a medical power of attorney allows the medical staff to talk with them and take their direction on medical decisions that need to be made.

Living Will or Advanced Directive

While a medical power of attorney names a person or persons to make medical decisions on another's behalf, the living will, also known as an advanced directive, leaves instructions for what is to be done if someone is terminally ill or permanently unconscious. Essentially, it gives instructions about a person's end-of-life circumstances.

Even if someone has a medical power of attorney, most states also ask for a living will or advanced directive document, or will want to see a provision in the medical power of attorney, to establish whether the person named is authorized to stop medical treatment in the event the client is terminally ill or permanently unconscious.

In the living will, specific instructions can be left for the person named, such as what to do in certain conditions—for example, whether to resuscitate or whether to use a feeding tube. This is an important document to have in place, because without it, the client may end up being treated when they don't want treatment.

Keep in mind that a separate living will with advanced directives may not be necessary if the language is incorporated into the medical power of attorney document.

It's not necessary to assign financial and medical powers of attorney to the same person. If a client has a daughter in the medical profession, she may be the best person to make medical decisions in the event of incapacitation. If a son is in the business world, he may be more suited to making financial decisions. Alternatively, both could be named in all decision processes because they will have different perspectives. Ultimately, assigning powers is an individual decision that should be based on the ability and trustworthiness of potential agents.

ESTATE PLAN COMPONENT TWO—WILLS AND TRUSTS

Wills and trusts determine what happens to your assets after you have passed on. These assets include bank accounts, investment accounts, retirement accounts, and life insurance policies as well as property, cars, furniture, jewelry, and other valuables. To stipulate what should happen to these assets, you need to work with your financial planner and estate planning attorney to ensure your assets are distributed according to your wishes. Depending on your wishes, this distribution may be handled by a simple will, or it may need the more detailed instruction that can be handled by a trust.

The Will

The first document that needs to be put in place for this component of the estate plan is the will. A will is a legal document by which an executor is named to manage the estate and provide for the distribution of a person's property upon their death according to the wishes laid out in the will.

A will is typically a short-term document that designates an asset to someone in a single direction—for example, leaving a house to a child. Once the executor of the will has retitled all the assets—for example, the bank account, or reregistering the house in the child's name per the direction of the will—the will is finished.

The first step in making a will is to list all your possessions. We talked in other sections about how everything starts with a detailed balance sheet of where a person stands financially. This is not just important for financial planning, but it is also important for estate planning. Creating a comprehensive list of assets helps to create the road map an estate planning attorney can follow to create the necessary documents to handle an estate according to the client's wishes.

Bank accounts should first be considered on this list: checking account, savings account, money market account, and CDs. How are these accounts currently titled? Are they held in one name only or jointly with spouses, children, or parents? How these accounts are titled determines how they pass to heirs after death. If they are held in the client's name only, it is possible to add transfer on death (TOD) or payable on death (POD) instructions. In this way, the bank automatically knows to give the assets in these accounts to the person or persons or to the trust named upon the owner's death.

It is also possible to add a TOD or POD to nonretirement investment accounts. These documents can stipulate a person or a trust to whom to transfer or pay the assets held in the account. In this way, the assets can be retitled from the owner's name to an individual or individuals or to the trust if the estate requires more robust management than can be handled by a will.

How to Think about Trusts

A trust is a legal entity that a client creates with the help of an estate planning attorney. The trust document names a trustee or trustees— that is, individuals who will handle the client's assets in accordance with specific instructions that are laid out in the trust document. In other words, these trustees handle the assets transferred into the trust on behalf of the client's beneficiaries.

Although the will can direct certain assets to the trust, the trust itself can be named as the beneficiary of life insurance policies, retirement accounts, bank accounts, or other assets. Many people have what is called a pour-over will, which simply states that all their assets go into the trust.

One of the major differences between a will and a trust is that the latter works over a longer period of time. If the beneficiary of all the assets is the trust, then the trust has long-term, more involved instructions on how the assets are to be distributed.

It is possible to get more granular about how assets are to be distributed. For example, they can be left to a child for their lifetime and then passed on to grandchildren thereafter. We have had many clients who are in second marriages, and both they and their spouses have children from first marriages. In one case, the husband wanted his estate to go to his second spouse upon his death, but upon his second wife's death, he wanted his assets to go to both his own children and her children (his stepchildren). This happens frequently with people who have raised their spouse's children. In this client's case, he wanted the children to benefit from the income generated from these assets during their lifetimes, but he then wanted the assets to pass to his grandchildren. Once he placed his assets in the trust, the will would be finished quickly upon his death, and the trust would take over to manage his assets for the long term.

Another reason to create a trust is to have creditor protection. For example, a trust allows a person to protect their assets from their beneficiaries' creditors, from lawsuits their beneficiaries face, or their business failures or divorces now and in the future.

If assets are held directly in the beneficiary's name, they can be subject to creditors. However, instead of leaving assets directly to a spouse, a brother, a sister, or children, if they are given to the trust, which is a separate legal entity from the beneficiary, the assets can be protected. Even if the assets are sold or the investments are changed, they are still owned by the trustees in trust for the benefit of the beneficiary. The beneficiary doesn't own the assets of the trust directly.

As clients are updating their estate plans, in many cases, their children have become responsible adults, more than capable of handling the money. Then the clients put a pencil to the amount of assets that they have accumulated. They have money in retirement accounts, individual investment accounts, oftentimes several million dollars in net worth. On top of that, they own some life insurance that will, on death, pay out a million dollars or more. They get hit by the bus, boom they're gone, and each of their three kids gets $1 million. Without a trust, I don't care how responsible your children are, the chances of their keeping the money are slim. How many kids know how to manage a million dollars? If you doubt me, ask yourself how many people who win the lottery manage to hang on to their millions. Believe me, your children won't be any different. Setting your money up in a trust is the first step if only because it makes that money a little less accessible. And if there's a cotrustee, you'll have a check and balance, when the child wants to spend $100,000 on that new Porsche. The cotrustee has a fiduciary duty to protect the money and do what's right.

None of us knows in advance how we're going to die. You can have the most financially responsible child in the world, but if you're shot and killed in a bank robbery or in a car accident, how will your children react in that moment of grief? None of us knows emotionally how our children will deal with that grief, and if you give that money to them directly, you run the risk of the money being squandered. You don't have a second chance.

Many people have a will and a trust; they don't want their children to get it all at one time. It might be a third of it now, a third five years later, and a third in ten years. The theory is if you blow the first third at twenty-five, you're still getting income until age thirty. If you blow the second third at age thirty, you still have some money left and some income from it until age thirty-five—and if you blow the final payment, you didn't deserve it in the first place. Like baseball, it's three strikes and you're out.

Because the trustee makes the distributions to the beneficiary, the trust can make sure they are benefiting the beneficiary and not the creditors. This kind of trust is referred to legally as a spendthrift trust. It protects assets from heirs who can't handle money or who may lose it on risky ventures. It allows people to make assets available to beneficiaries to provide them with health, support, maintenance, and education, for example, but not to pay their creditors. In this way, it is possible to ensure assets will eventually be passed to grandchildren.

An important point to remember regarding creditor protection is that the financial planner or estate planning attorney should make sure the assets going into the trust do not go through the will first. The POD or the TOD come into effect first upon death; therefore, the TOD and POD should specify the trust as beneficiary in order to prevent the assets from landing in the estate. Whatever assets are not directed in this way will become part of the probate estate. The probate court has jurisdiction over assets that go through probate court, and these may be subject to creditor claims. However, assets that are set up to pass directly into the trust are not subject to these claims.

3 COMMON PLANNING MISTAKES

Clearly, estate planning is far more involved than simply making out a will.

By far the most common problem we see is people doing nothing. Without properly drafted wills and trusts, your heirs or beneficiaries can run into trouble. Without a will, the distribution of assets will be subject to the rules of the state in which the owner lived. These rules may have no relationship to what the owner would like to see happen to his or her assets. In addition, passing assets to the people designated by the state can be an expensive and time-consuming process. The family could end up having to buy a fiduciary bond as required by the probate court to guarantee that whoever is taking care of the money or assets is fulfilling their duties and not—for example, stealing money from the

> By far the most common problem we see is people doing nothing.

rest of the family. The family could end up in probate court in a time-consuming and expensive process that could have been avoided had you drafted a will.

Another common problem is failing to correctly title accounts. Although an estate planning attorney can prepare all the estate planning documents, review them with their clients, and then prepare final signature copies, the greatest documents in the world won't help if the titling of the assets doesn't mirror what the client is trying to accomplish. If a person dies without a will but added beneficiary designations on the retirement plans or designated a beneficiary on the life insurance policy, these assets will pass to the heirs without going through the probate courts. With a will, however, it is important to update the beneficiaries on these accounts. People often update their will after a divorce or remarriage, for example, but fail to change the designation on their retirement accounts and insurance policy to match the wishes of their revised will. In this situation, the designation on the accounts may take precedence over the will, meaning an inheritance will be passed that is not in compliance with the client's revised wishes.

This is why it is important that the financial planner takes over from the estate planning attorney once the documents are signed to make sure the assets are properly titled and will flow to the trust upon the owner's death in a way that is consistent with the instructions in the documents. In this way, a carefully crafted and coordinated estate planning road map will exist and continue to be updated to make sure the client's wishes are followed when he or she dies.

Another common mistake people make is writing a simple will. Very often, people make a will when their children are born to name a guardian in case they die prematurely. This is important to stipulate when the children are young, but, as you've already seen in this chapter, there are many more details involved in estate planning. Circumstances also change. A plan that worked twenty years ago will not suffice today. Most people acquire assets, their income is likely significantly higher, they may have received an inheritance, and their children may no longer be minors. A twenty-year-old estate plan will need rigorous updating.

Finally, as mentioned earlier, failing to think about the lifetime planning component of an estate plan is a common mistake. It is important to have individuals named with financial and medical powers of attorney available in the event of incapacitation, and it is also vital that a living will or end-of-life directive language be in place so that end-of-life wishes are respected and clients don't risk being subjected to unwanted, life-prolonging treatments.

A WORD ON TAXATION

Many people think of their tax burden and about ways to offset taxes in their estate plans. However, it is more important to establish first what someone wants to accomplish and then look at the tax rules. This is particularly true since the new tax rules came into effect that increased the federal tax-exempt limit on estate taxes to $11.7 million per individual starting in 2021. The state threshold varies, but in many states, including currently Ohio, there is no estate tax. These rules are subject to change in 2026, but for now, these limits make the tax planning part of estate planning of little concern for most people.

However, there is one caveat. Although every individual can pass on at least $11.7 million free of inheritance or estate taxes, this is not necessarily free of income taxes if some of those assets are pretax retirement accounts or in an annuity contract. Beneficiaries will be subject to income tax when the money is pulled out of those accounts. Therefore, income tax planning plays a role in how assets are passed along. Beneficiaries should discuss this with their financial planners before withdrawing funds to ensure they are following the best tax strategies available.

For individuals leaving estates of more than $11.7 million who are philanthropically inclined, some advanced planning strategies exist that can help offset the tax burden and benefit their charities of choice. Setting up charitable foundations or donating stock or other appreciated assets to charities offers ways to sidestep the estate tax and possibly income tax. Financial planners will be able to offer effective gifting options for people who are interested in giving back.

TAKEAWAY

→ If something happened to you today, what would you want to have happen to everything you own?

→ The answer should include a comprehensive road map that stipulates how instructions have been put in place to accomplish those wishes. To create this road map, you should work with an estate planning attorney and a financial planner who specializes in this area and make sure they are working in tandem.

→ A comprehensive estate plan should include a will and trusts and a current financial and medical power of attorney along with living will directives. You should review these documents every three or four years to make sure they reflect changes in your lifestyle. Pay careful attention to all assets and how those assets are titled to make sure that they are consistent with how they should be passed to heirs.

→ An estate plan is also the perfect vehicle with which to leave a legacy. Many people look back on what they have accumulated throughout their lifetimes. They have been fortunate enough to amass some wealth, and they want to give something back. A charitable bequest can be included in any estate plan, either directly or through a trust or a foundation. This gives every investor the opportunity to leave a legacy.

→ Here's one of the most important takeaways from this chapter. Many people have the misconception that trusts are only for the wealthy. In the old days, it was to avoid estate taxes when you die. Today, with the higher exemption limits, it's to preserve your estate for your children and your grandchildren, to create a legacy and to protect your children and grandchildren from themselves.

We're not just put on this earth to make money and pass it on so that our loved ones can inherit that money, make more, and pass it on. Next, I'm going to share with you a topic that's especially important to me. We've touched on leaving a legacy many times in this book. Now let's look at legacies, along with ways you can give back.

CHAPTER 13

Giving Back

Giving back is a cornerstone of my personal belief system and of our corporate culture. As I mentioned earlier in this book, my parents always found it in their hearts to give something back to the church. They gave my brother and me some change to put in the basket in church every Sunday so that we adopted these values too. They were not well off, but if somebody in the church was in need, my mother baked something for them. In this way, despite not having much, I grew up in an environment of giving, and this influenced me into adulthood and even today.

However, I have found that there are givers and takers in the world; the former always help, and the latter can often take to the point of entitlement. They believe the world owes them something rather than believing in hard work and doing the best they can. They can be draining. More often than not, they do not do much to help themselves get ahead. It is easier to hold out a hand and accept from others.

That said, hardworking people can end up in unfortunate circumstances and sometimes need a helping hand to get back on their feet. They do not want to end up living on charity or developing a dependency on others.

My philosophy on giving is based on the belief that, as the saying goes, if you give a poor man a fish, you feed him for a day, but if you teach him to fish, you give him an occupation that will feed him for a lifetime. It is important to give back, but it is also important that what you give constitutes real and lasting help. This has colored which people and foundations I support. I have made it a mission to become involved in causes and charities so that I can offer a helping hand and give to those who want to get back on their feet.

The upside of having the six pieces of a financial plan in place is that it gives you the time, resources, and stability, especially in retirement, to give back and be a positive influence in the community. This chapter looks at how people can be an effective force for good by looking at knowledge sharing, contributing to veteran and community support, providing medical and health support to those who need it, and ultimately, leaving a legacy of which they can be proud.

LIFE IS A LABYRINTH

Grace Cathedral, an Episcopal Church in San Francisco, has a replica of the Chartres Labyrinth that people can walk. It has only one way in and one way out, making the labyrinth a journey. The year before my mother-in-law passed, we took an adventure- and sightseeing-filled vacation to the West Coast, her first and only trip there. At Grace Cathedral, she experienced the labyrinth for herself.

The labyrinth in Grace Cathedral
David.Clay.Photography / CC BY-SA
(https://creativecommons.org/licenses/by-sa/4.0)

In France, in the Christian tradition, walking the labyrinth represents a holy pilgrimage, a journey within which lives a larger spiritual quest. These walks are good as a nondenominational cross-cultural practice for well-being. The labyrinth can be walked to find balance, meditate, or quiet one's mind. Some walk it in celebration, some in sadness, and others in search of healing.

Life is like a labyrinth. The single entrance and exit of the labyrinth, its twists and turns, and what a person does along the way do make a difference. Every twist or a turn is a decision that has to be made. A certain amount of skill can make a person successful, but there is also a certain amount of luck. There is only one way in and one way out. Between those two absolutes, life is filled with twists and turns, choices and decisions, and the need to take ownership for both the decisions that we make and the resulting consequences.

The labyrinth reminds us that it is important to prepare for what might be around the corner. A person can go to a doctor for a routine physical and find a serious problem that the doctor must try to cure and then follow up. Financial planning is similar. It is a lifelong journey, which means an advisor's relationship with a client is a lifetime's journey. This journey should continue after one or the other is gone, which is why our firm shares its core philosophy and beliefs and takes a consistent approach across all our advisors, so that it will continue to serve clients and look out for their best interests.

The idea of walking the journey of life with our clients is so integral to our philosophy of thinking in terms of quality of life that I donated money to build a labyrinth at the small Episcopal Church on an island called Put-In-Bay on Lake Erie in northern Ohio. This was my mother-in-law's home, and she attended that church. We arranged for the landscaper to build it, and we continue to provide funds to have it maintained. Prior to COVID, the island attracted a lot of tourists, and the labyrinth hopefully prompts reflection among those who journey through it.

KNOWLEDGE SHARING

For the last twenty years, Chornyak & Associates has run a monthly luncheon for people who are in job transition. When corporations terminate an employee, executive, or middle management employee, they often provide them with outplacement services as part of their severance package. These services allow the terminated employee to work with an organization that specializes in helping them transition from that job to finding a new one. This can involve writing resumes to counseling to identifying what the best career paths might be for them based on their skill sets and backgrounds. They also have opportunities to network with other individuals in the same situation and meet new corporate leaders.

> Life is like a labyrinth... there is only one way in and only one way out.

People in job transition need to make financial decisions, such as what to do with the group benefits, life insurance, disability insurance, their 401(k), and the health insurance they had with their previous employer. They may get severance equal to three, six, or twelve months of compensation, which may be paid in a normal pay cycle or as a lump sum. In all these situations, the terminated employee needs to plan but doesn't know what to do, especially while still grappling emotionally with the loss of their job.

To help them, I reached out to one of the outplacement organizations in Columbus and suggested we invite them to a luncheon. During this luncheon, we talked to them as a group about the financial issues ahead and answered any questions they had.

Most people in the workplace spend their waking hours doing the best job that they can, and when they are not at work, they want to spend time with their families. They neglect managing their finances, so when they get into a transitional phase of their life, such as periods of unemployment, they do not know how to start thinking about money. At our lunches, we share our philosophy about what to do with their 401(k), group life insurance, wills and trusts, and medical and financial powers of attorney. One advantage of job transition is that it provides you with downtime, which is an opportunity to tackle finances before landing a new job and becoming preoccupied again.

One common piece of advice we give at these luncheons relates to income tax. When people are going through job transition, they often get their severance pay in a lump sum rather than continuing their normal pay cycle for three to six months. Payroll withholding rules require employers to withhold a higher percentage from the severance check if it is a larger lump sum. Therefore, when people are in job transition, oftentimes more money is withheld for federal and state taxes than will actually be owed when they file their tax return the next year. This can be compensated for by claiming additional deductions when you find a new position, so that your take-home pay is higher and your refund will be lower. This helps to smooth out your cash flow.

Similarly, if someone loses their job early in the year and has three months of severance, their income tax bill in April will be lower because their income is significantly lower. Therefore, we suggest that they adjust their withholding on their weekly, biweekly, or monthly severance check. If they increase their deductions, they will have less withheld because they are going to owe less tax when they eventually file. This gives them more take-home pay, which they can put away to help them ride through the storm until they find a new position.

At a luncheon seminar, one woman said she usually gets a $4,000 or $5,000 refund between federal and state taxes each year. I suggested she adjust her withholdings for the six months of her severance pay. This would make her refund lower, but it would give her the cash now when she needed it most while in job transition.

In job transition, when the next job is still unknown, that money is better as cash in the job seeker's pocket—rather than the government's pocket. The government needs to be paid only what it is owed, not more, and certainly not so much that a big refund is due the next year when one's cash flow is tight now while unemployed. With that small change in the woman's deductions, she had $5,000 more in her pocket when she needed it.

In conjunction with these luncheons, if people are interested in more specific advice, they can meet with us for a two-hour pro bono counseling session to review some of their financial documents. We review their financial situation and help point them in the right direction. This is not a high-pressure, high-pitch meeting to get them to do business with us. As I mentioned earlier, I believe when you give unconditionally, it comes back tenfold. In this case of giving by sharing knowledge, some of them stayed with us to manage their long-term financial plans, so we gained some new clients in the process.

SUPPORTING THE COMMUNITY

Our firm sponsors Boy Scout programs throughout the year. The husband of one of our employees was in charge of the Boy Scout Organization for central Ohio, and through him, we became familiar with the group's work.

The Boy Scouts' value system is consistent with my own, and I admire the values it instills in its young members. Their pledge— "On my honor, I will do my best to do my duty to God and my country and to obey the Scout Law; to help other people at all times; to keep myself physically strong, mentally awake, and morally straight"—reflects the values I adopted growing up. It is consistent with my belief about how people should be treated. I also appreciate the character-building value inherent in the process of earning badges and rewards for meeting certain goals and achievements.

When the Boy Scouts had their annual trap shoot fundraiser, we sponsored the event. It was a way of helping the Scouts raise money, and at the same time, it exposed some of our other clients to the Scout's organization, and now they donate money or time as well.

In addition to the Boy Scouts, I have supported National Public Radio for many years. It broadcasts good stories. Some I agree with, and some I do not agree with, but both give me a perspective, which is important in life. Therefore, our company supports and sponsors the local public radio station. Aside from its in-depth stories, our local NPR station features the music of local artists and supports local high school and college students who are interested in a career path in broadcasting through work experience and mentoring.

When NPR has its on-air fundraisers, which it does several times a year, the hosts ask listeners to make a commitment to help support the station. In the beginning, I made personal donations, but we soon became one of the small local businesses that sponsored programs throughout the year. In exchange for our support, the station says, "This program is being brought to you in part by Chornyak & Associates, a local financial planning firm." I later expanded this into matching donations for a set period of time on a given day. The station then went on air and announced, "We have a special donation program right now, offered by Chornyak & Associates. If you call in between 4:00 and 7:00 today, they will match your donation dollar for dollar." This inspired other people to call in and double the donation. It was a great success. My son even went down to the station during the matching hour and went on the air and said, "Please call in now. Take my Dad's money." It was fun. It was a way of giving back that mobilized the community and allowed the station to meet its fundraising needs when it was struggling, and it was a great way to contribute to the community.

We also support the Dublin Arts Council in the Dublin, Ohio, community in a variety of ways. The arts council provides concerts by local artists every Sunday evening during the summer, and once a year at its spring gala, it holds a silent auction with cocktails and hors d'oeuvres to raise money to support this and other ventures. Many years ago, one of our clients, an attorney who sat on the arts council's board of directors, approached me and asked if we'd be interested in attending the silent auction. We became a corporate sponsor, and I invited a dozen clients to come along and buy something in the auction to support the council. It was a huge success, and it has now become an annual event at our firm.

VETERANS SUPPORT

A few years ago, a client and old friend drew my attention to the plight of veterans. Many people who served our country came back wounded and ended up with lifelong problems or disabilities. He wanted to sponsor a Wounded Warrior program and asked for my help.

My father and uncles fought in World War II. I have clients who served and others who lost brothers in Vietnam. War changes people. It affects people. I have much respect for the men and women in the armed forces who help protect us.

One of the Wounded Warrior programs is called Healing Waters. In this program, the local Veterans Administration (VA) organizes local fishing trips where they can meet other Wounded Warriors.

We decided to sponsor two Wounded Warriors brothers on a trip to Alaska to fly-fish, something they would probably never otherwise experience. The VA put us in touch with the two brothers who served in Iraq on several tours of duty; both of them had resulting disabilities. They were fine young men, raised in Dayton, Ohio, by their mother after their father died. We took them to Alaska with us on our annual fly-fishing trip, and they had the time of their lives.

It was a wonderful experience to get to know them, to hear about their struggles and how they served our country. Our Alaska fishing trip was a way to give something back to a couple of Wounded Warriors.

HEALTH AND MEDICAL GIVING

My son, who is also a financial planner at Chornyak & Associates, is very active in Pelotonia, which raises funds for innovative cancer research at The Ohio State University Comprehensive Cancer Center. My son takes part in its one-hundred-mile-a-day bike ride to raise money. Some of our clients also cycle in the fundraising effort, and we provide matching dollars. Similarly, my niece does a sixty-mile walk in three days for the Susan G. Komen breast cancer foundation.

As a company, we are involved in making donations to Pelotonia, and many of our clients have also become directly involved in supporting the nonprofit organization. This often happens when somebody has a parent, brother, sister, or other relative who has either suffered with or died of cancer, and they see firsthand the distress of that disease. We are all committed to supporting cancer research, both through Pelotonia and through Susan G. Komen.

Recently, Alexandra Armstrong, an old friend and a nationally renowned and highly respected Certified Financial Planner, certified since the 1970s, told me of a new program in which the Foundation for Financial Planning hoped to raise $1.5 million to provide pro bono financial planning to families dealing with cancer. It needed help with issues from housing to paying bills and covering medical costs. It was a pilot program that was just getting off the ground and was in need of corporate sponsors. Her company had donated $25,000. I read the literature she provided and donated $50,000. When she heard what I had donated, she called and said, "I need to up my game. I'm contributing another $25,000." I was pleased to hear that my effort was not only personally rewarding but that it inspired someone else to donate more.

When I have friends and clients who are givers, giving money and time and expertise, I want to support their efforts too.

Two other health-related foundations we support are the Make-a-Wish Foundation and the Arthritis Foundation. We became involved in another nonprofit venture when a joint implant surgeon client who was part of the practice of a leading hip and knee practice came to us. Each year, he goes to a third-world country with a team of physicians and nurses to perform hip and knee surgeries for people there who are in dire need of medical care and treatment. It is an expensive undertaking, so we donate a significant amount of money to contribute to their effort to give back.

I have a friend whose father was battling cancer a few years ago. The family had modest means, and the illness devastated them. The father wanted to stay at home, which meant his wife and two children had to try to take care of him. They all had jobs, and the effort was draining them. They needed relief. One of our clients owns a home healthcare company in Columbus, so I explained that the man had only four to six weeks left to live and asked if they could help and send me the bill. They arranged for someone to go in and sit with him eight hours a day, three days a week. For the next few weeks, until the father passed, the family had some well-needed respite. Helping them was immensely gratifying.

There are always limitations to the amount we can give, but I have learned that it is always good to give what you can to people and organizations to which you relate, where the benefits to society, to the community, to the individual, and to the family are evident.

Giving back is not just about giving to an organization. My career has helped place me in a good financial position to be of help, but sometimes it is valuable to directly help someone in need. This allows you to connect with the receiver of the gift. It is not always about paying someone's bill. Sometimes it is about giving them food or providing a car they cannot afford, or something that helps to improve the quality of their life.

LEGACY

Giving is not just monetary. It is giving of yourself in myriad ways. One of the greatest gifts that can be bestowed on a child is to teach them the value of giving. This is one way to leave a legacy.

> One of the greatest gifts that can be bestowed on a child is to teach them the value of giving. This is one way to leave a legacy.

I built a business based on years of real-life experience in asking clients lots of questions to get to know them as much as I could, so that I could give advice based on one core principle: If I were in their shoes, what steps would I take? This is how I have always given advice and always will. I have mentored those around me to give advice in this way. This is the only real and effective way to give advice, and I hope that as our firm continues, that core principle will remain intact.

We have helped some clients set up charitable foundations and name their children as the trustees of that foundation. While they are alive, they put seed money into the foundation, and upon their deaths, the fund is split between the children to donate to their charity of choice. This is a wonderful way to leave a legacy, not just in monetary terms but in terms of instilling the spirit of giving in future generations. Teaching the next generation the value of giving is a true and valuable legacy.

Giving without expecting anything in return offers a great sense of satisfaction. Giving out of obligation can leave a bad taste in the mouth, as does being pressured to give because someone has a sense of entitlement. We should give not because it is required but because we are moved to do so. Many years ago, I helped manage the investments for several church endowment funds on the condition that my compensation was to be donated back to the church. Like my mother had done with her skill set, I wanted to take my knowledge and expertise and give it back.

When I think of legacy, I also think of those who have passed. When my mother passed in 1995, I wrote her eulogy. I reflected on stories she told us that made us who we are today. Too often, we do not thank the people who helped get us to where we are. We would probably be better people if we imagined writing a eulogy to those still living who have touched our lives. We should decide what we would write and then go to that person and share it. Many people have gifted me with their help. Many people, such as my mother, have gifted me with their legacy. Sometimes we forget that expressing our gratitude is giving back too. Sometimes giving back can be as simple as asking yourself, "How am I touching people's lives today? Is it in a positive way or a negative way?"

TAKEAWAY

→ Being in a position to help is uplifting. I do not expect, want, or need a thank-you because I'm grateful that I have been blessed in my life. As mentioned earlier, what we give comes back tenfold.

→ I have always believed it's important to treat people the way you want to be treated yourself. This way, you never need to say you are sorry.

→ It is important to be kind and considerate of others. It is important to be honest and have integrity in your word. It is important to be polite to all people. It is important to finish what you start, but it is equally important to recognize that you are never finished. You never stop.

→ The giving should continue long after you are gone. In my case, I have established a company that is imbued with these values that I hope will be my legacy to future generations.

→ I hope that my staff, my clients, and my family will continue to give. I hope I have helped them have a better understanding and appreciation of the value of giving. I hope that somewhere along the way, long after I'm gone, they may reflect back and say, "What would Joe do?" and then give with their hearts.

ACKNOWLEDGMENTS

I'm grateful to the following individuals who have taught me so much over the years and have helped me become the person I am today. Their input and guidance have helped shape this book.

My son, Joe Chornyak Jr.

My brother, Mike Chornyak

Steve Deschenes and everyone at American Funds

My niece, Lisa Fisher

Bill Heffner

Bob Mauk

Bob Pappas

My longtime clients, who have placed their faith and trust in me

My entire staff, who are like family to me

The many excellent tax professionals I've worked with over the years

My dear friend Alex Armstrong

Lee Brower and Dan Sullivan and everyone at Strategic Coach

My thanks to everyone at Advantage|ForbesBooks, including my editor, Bonnie Hearn Hill. And to the memory of my dear friend Bill Reichert.

ABOUT THE AUTHOR

With more than forty years of experience in the financial planning field, Joe Chornyak is the managing partner of Chornyak & Associates in Columbus, Ohio, managing over $1.3 billion in assets for more than a thousand individuals and businesses nationwide. His financial advisory philosophy is based upon broad investment diversification, conservative risk taking, and a thorough and disciplined approach based on one simple belief: investors rarely reap above-average returns by taking unnecessary risks. He sees himself as his clients' true partner and provides advice that he personally uses to manage his own financial affairs. He is committed to helping others avoid pitfalls and secure their financial futures. Joe has been licensed in the securities industry since 1978 and has been a Certified Financial Planner since 1982. Over the years, he has been named among the nation's top investment advisors by *Forbes, Barron's,* and *Financial Times.*

OUR SERVICES

If you have found the information in this book helpful and would like to know more about our services, please feel free to contact us.

Chornyak & Associates
www.chornyak.com
614-888-2121